The Fabian Society

The Fabian Society is Britain's leading left of centre think tank and political society, committed to creating the political ideas and policy debates which can shape the future of progressive politics.

With over 300 Fabian MPs, MEPs, Peers, MSPs and AMs, the Society plays an unparalleled role in linking the ability to influence policy debates at the highest level with vigorous grassroots debate among our growing membership of over 7000 people, 70 local branches meeting regularly throughout Britain and a vibrant Young Fabian section organising its own activities. Fabian publications, events and ideas therefore reach and influence a wider audience than those of any comparable think tank. The Society is unique among think tanks in being a thriving, democratically-constituted membership organisation, affiliated to the Labour Party but organisationally and editorially independent.

For over 120 years Fabians have been central to every important renewal and revision of left of centre thinking. The Fabian commitment to open and participatory debate is as important today as ever before as we explore the ideas, politics and policies which will define the next generation of progressive politics in Britain, Europe and around the world. To find out more about the Fabian Society, the Young Fabians, the Fabian Women's Network and our local societies, please visit our web site at **www.fabians.org.uk**.

Joining the Fabians is easy
For more information about joining the Fabian Society and to learn more about our recent publications, please turn to **page 89**.

Fabian Society
11 Dartmouth Street
London SW1H 9BN
www.fabians.org.uk

 Fabian ideas 625
Editorial Director: Tom Hampson
Editorial Manager: Ed Wallis

First published 2009

ISBN 9 780 7163 0625 2

We would especially like to thank TUFM and Groundwork for their generous support.

British Library Cataloguing in Publication data.
A catalogue record for this book is available from the British Library.

Printed and bound by DG3

The Green Crunch
Why we need a new economics for Britain's environmental challenge

Sir John Harman

Contents

Preface
Meeting the progressive challenge

This pamphlet deals with big environmental challenges and how they impact on politics. The truth is that the practical politics are often hard to handle. For example, this winter we are likely to see gas and electricity bills rising rapidly in response to wholesale markets and to the price of oil. Those who will feel this most are the poor, but it will hurt a significant proportion of the electorate, compounding the problems of recession and job insecurity caused by the mayhem in the financial sector.

- **The Government has often been unable to meet this challenge**
  It has seemed almost impossible to get popular support to meet the environmental challenge head on when there is a cost involved – as we have seen with the fuel duty protests, in road pricing, in aviation. In ten years, and with a couple of creditable exceptions like the land-fill tax escalator, there has been very little actual use of the tax system in the way Gordon Brown promised in 1997. For all political parties it seems there is always a reason to avoid the green challenge.

- **What is Labour's strategy for tomorrow's economy?**
  We have seen the end of the era of artificially low commodity prices, but you wouldn't know it. The economic conditions of the late 20th century are a thing of the past and a successful 21st century economy will look quite different. What is being done to prepare Britain for this future?

■ **2009 is an important year**
This is a make-or-break year for a global climate deal. And this will only succeed if reflected in national politics. Crucially, the destabilising consequences of the recession can be used as a way of accelerating the transition to a greener, more resource-efficient economy, which also serves the nation's long-term comparative advantage.

John Harman's pamphlet follows the logic of the environmental challenge into these and other aspects of policy and politics. By turns sobering and optimistic, strategic and pragmatic, his analysis delivers messages for policy-makers, politicians, and for the Labour Party.

Tom Hampson
Editorial Director
The Fabian Society

The Green Crunch
Messages to politicians

- **Government is failing to communicate to voters**
  The government Chief Scientist may have the ear of the decision-makers but Jeremy Clarkson has the ear of the electorate. Westminster is convinced of the challenge, but the public perception is far less coherent. Politicians must put the environmental facts squarely into the mainstream of electoral politics before voters will really respond.

- **As a result, rising costs are political dynamite**
  It is extremely unlikely that we will ever get back to the retail energy prices of the last 15 years or so. This fact is not being squarely presented to the electorate. The way in which we have communicated our political objectives means voters see rising energy costs as a failure of politics.

- **Learning from Obama how to make the case**
  Barack Obama won, in the gas-addicted USA, with an energy programme that used worries over oil security to mobilise support for a drive towards renewables and energy efficiency and at the same time the creation of new jobs.

- **We need a new politics**
  In Britain, we must embed an ecological understanding into our political principles and to accept that the management of our place in the natural world is as important a political purpose as economic or social management.

- **We must be determinedly internationalist**
  We must build up the power of global institutions for the really global issues but do not allow them to use that power to invade the decisions which can and should be made at national level.

- **Green politics has got it wrong and must embrace globalisation**
  Internationalism is a rational approach to risk reduction. In this the instincts of traditional green politics towards insularity and self-sufficiency are completely mistaken. Any true green politics must see globalisation as more opportunity than threat.

- **Government must not try to control everything**
  This Government must continue the existing shift from government as an exercise in command-and-control to one of ensuring accountability. It is right to place power at the level where it can most effectively be used for any given objective – the subsidiarity principle – and that level can be above or below the nation state.

- **Subsidiarity is the key**
  'Subsidiarity' is a word to avoid, but it is an essential principle for Labour if we wish to sidestep the risk of the collective swamping the individual, or of new institutions being undemocratic. It means devolution *upwards* in a society where the source of political authority is the individual and not the state.

- **Eurosceptics have held back our progress**
  Westminster's obsession with national sovereignty has been allowed to muddy our politics in this country for far too long. We need new political institutions beyond the state, which must satisfy the demands of accountability and justice and do not erode but support individual rights and freedoms.

- **There is a real appetite for leadership**
  The electorate, not the political class, must define and demand the change we need. And although they are unlikely to do so very quickly without political leadership, we are at the point at which such leadership would find a positive response.

Messages to Labour

- **Labour can be the vehicle for environmentally intelligent politics**
  The fundamental instincts and strengths of the Labour movement – equality, the priority given to the common interest, internationalism – could make it the most promising existing vehicle for this new politics.

- **Voters' instincts can be with Labour**
  Collective action for the collective good should be – is – natural Labour ground, and it is one that not only makes absolute sense in terms of enlightened self-interest in the face of ecological pressures but also one that has enduring appeal to the British electorate.

- **This isn't about a red-green coalition**
  Labour need not strain to recruit green votes into some sort of red-green alliance by adopting minority issues., There are many aspects of current green politics – especially its attitude to science – that are dangerously irrelevant.

- **We must get our messages right**
  An ecologically intelligent politics cannot be smuggled past the electorate. We need a better message than "if we don't take action, things will get a lot worse" – a political movement cannot e built on the platform of making the best of a bad job.

Messages to policy-makers

■ **Industrial transition**
We must decouple wealth creation from resource depletion. This will change the industrial structure of Britain, create and destroy jobs, require new technologies, products and processes to evolve.

■ **A new economics**
For most of its 200 year history, economics has effectively assumed that what environmental scientists call 'sources' and 'sinks' are to all intents and purposes infinite. This cannot continue. We need an economics rooted in physical & biological science.

■ **We need to manage the transition**
The development of the analytical tools and economic theory to support a new economics has to be an urgent priority for government, and we need a transition strategy to get us from where we are to where we need to be.

■ **We need to manage carbon targets directly**
Carbon pricing by itself cannot deliver 80 per cent decarbonisation. The market alone cannot be relied on and it is clear that there has also to be a regulatory response, so that policy will have to manage carbon targets directly as well as managing price.

■ **We need a package of carbon measures**
We need much more rapid decarbonisation, heavily incentivised by government, more certainty over future carbon price to stabilise investment behaviours and measures to preserve affordability for individual consumers.

■ **The right mix of tools**

We must be prepared to use a range of tools: price control; social tariffs; an industrial strategy linking heavy public sector support for new technologies to private investment planning; the tax system to manage the price trajectory against a backdrop of fluctuating global wholesale markets, recycling a variable tax take into subsidy for industrial transition or social tariffs.

■ **Low carbon energy must include nuclear**

At some point soon we hope to have a mix of low or zero-carbon generation. This must include nuclear, probably a proportion of coal with carbon capture, and much greater recovery and use of heat in the generating process, either local or national.

■ **Personal carbon allowances are too authoritarian**

The interest that the Government is showing in personal carbon allowances is worrying. Until there are alternative low-carbon behaviours and products available, personal carbon rationing would be an essentially authoritarian intervention. The left needs to offer a more liberal version of collective action.

■ **The ecological challenge can be won in the cities**

For the first time more than 50 per cent of the Earth's human population lives in cities. How our cities function as environmental communities is central. For it is in the organisation of urban life – its transport patterns, its demands on energy, water, food, materials etc – that the real opportunity lies for finding ways of reducing our average impact on nature. If the city can become successful in ecological terms, we will have won the battle.

The Green Crunch

Introduction

I was unbelievably lucky in when and where I was born. So, probably, were you. The last 50 years in this country, and in the developed world as a whole, have been years of widespread and unprecedented well-being in material wealth, in health, in security. Perhaps that good fortune is why it has taken so long for the penny to drop: that the means by which this bounty has been won cannot be sustained indefinitely. We are depleting our natural capital, and we need to do something about it.

That realisation has become widespread in the first years of the new century, yet it was only very recently a minority concern. The evidence has been there, the science is well-known, but it is uncomfortable evidence and we have not seen the need to admit it, nor have we welcomed those who tried to draw it to our attention.[1] And as a result, politics has found it hard to deal with.

This pamphlet starts with the proposition that we are in trouble with our place on the planet. This tends to have been presented as a series of technical challenges but it seems to me to be much more than that; it is also a profound political challenge which cannot be met within the social/economic framework which has dominated all Western politics in my lifetime. In the pamphlet, I say: "We stand before a new imperative; that of creating a politics which meets our ecological as well as our social and economic needs."

So this is a call to embed an ecological understanding into our political principles and to accept that the management of our place in the natural world is as important a political purpose as economic or social management.

1

Where does that lead us? This is the practical political question that I want to explore in this pamphlet. It is not a manifesto or a green tract.

I want instead to follow the logic of the proposition to understand at least some of the political principles that it brings in its wake; I want to relate those principles to a few of the difficult issues now facing Government; and I want to consider what they mean for the politics of the left in Britain, principally of course for Labour. Above all, because I regard our political processes and institutions as a vital part of our species intelligence, I want others – I want you – to engage in this effort to think through how we will use them to respond to the ecological challenge that indubitably faces us.

Politics need not be wary of this challenge but can embrace it, indeed be refreshed by it. There could, after all, be nothing more relevant than this to our lives in the unfolding century. The question isn't whether there will be change but whether it will be anticipated, managed, understood in time.

What changes? There seem to me to be several which are both significant in their difficulty and yet inseparable from the logic of the position.

The economic challenge
In economics, our dominant models will be – already are – an inadequate tool for the understanding of what I will term the economics of nature, and policy will have to be informed by a wider analysis of natural capital and the flows of natural resources through the human economy.

The fairness challenge
The pricing of many resources will create problems of equity in the short term. In the longer term, we will need greater intervention in markets, and our idea of equity will have to include people's access to natural resources.

The international challenge
These problems of fairness will have a big impact on international affairs and will require much more determined internationalism. In particular there will be a need for stronger international institutions and law to manage our ecological impact.

The democratic challenge

The problem raises a question over the role of the nation state. It can keep its place as the unit of government with the primary electoral mandate but within a wider spectrum of competences at other levels. There will also need to be some long-term policy objectives that are managed outside the electoral cycle.

The growth challenge

Changes in the way we use resources will both destroy existing economic activities and create new ones. Our comparative advantage as a nation will depend critically on having the right industrial strategy and being able to give the correct priority to long-term benefits over short-term costs. This means giving reliable, bankable, long-term signals on resource pricing. Any return to growth which fails to begin this industrial transition will itself be transitory.

One of the problems faced by politicians of all parties today is that any one of these themes, taken in isolation, creates significant electoral resistance. That is why it is quite rational to be pessimistic about our chances of finding a political settlement which ensures sustainable well-being. Only if politics explicitly faces the ecological realities on the same level and with the same gravity as it faces social and economic realities will it carry conviction; but then it will also justify optimism.

This can be a politics of equity, of collective action in the collective interest, internationalist and liberal; resonant in so many ways to the instincts of Labour. That doesn't mean that Labour will naturally rise to the challenge. But I pray that it will.

John Harman
December 2008

The Green Crunch

1. Paradigm lost

Back in September 2008, Britain was returning, damply, from holiday, and politics was resuming with the Conference season. The talk was all of economic downturn, the credit crunch, rising prices and the impact this winter of soaring energy costs on the poor; or rather, on practically everyone. The issue of the day within the Labour Party was how the Government could alleviate at least some of this pain, whether it should do so by imposing a special tax on the energy companies and whether to use any new money for long-term solutions or immediate palliatives.

By the year's end, politics has changed almost out of recognition. The credit crunch has reared up into a worldwide financial crisis, major banks in Europe and America have been nationalised, interest rates slashed and we face a recession of uncertain depth and duration. The longest period of uninterrupted growth in modern history has come to an abrupt end. Meanwhile the Government's public standing is recovering on the back of its handling of the economic crisis. While the world holds its breath, commodity prices have fallen back and some of the sting has gone out of the summer's price worries. Some, but not all. Oil may be less than half the price it was in July, but it is still at historically high levels.

Will normal business be resumed? If so, when? And what will happen to prices when it is?

It will be quite a while before we know how this story unfolds, though events are moving so quickly that by the time you read this, we will certainly know more of the plot. The scale of the crisis is the product of a number of loosely related pressures – the political cycle, the economic cycle, even the weather – acting at the same time. These pressures test the resolve and capacity of governments, which are judged by how they respond.

So is this just the stuff of day-to-day politics, of, "events, dear boy, events"?

I doubt it. 'Events' certainly are at play, and the financial storm is present and serious; but so is something else, something much more long-lasting, more real, yet so staringly obvious that we don't pay attention to it, and for which our politics is unbelievably ill-prepared; and that is the incompatibility of our patterns of economic behaviour with the physical and biological systems on which they depend. This pamphlet explores the underlying problem and what it might mean for politics, especially for the politics of the Labour movement and the left here in Britain, but also at a global level.

This is no longer just an issue of science and how science informs political decisions. What we saw emerging in the summer's red-top headlines about food and fuel prices, now half-forgotten in the financial *mêlée*, is not a theoretical argument but the very real impact of something entirely predictable: the end of the era of artificially low commodity prices. For we can say with some certainty that the costs of oil and other fossil fuels, and of grain, metals and other raw materials, are on rising trends. Even if you reject the ecological basis of this trend you can simply apply the laws of supply and demand. As I write this, many commodity prices have come off the highs that they hit earlier in the year. The memory of the price shocks may fade but the longer term trends are there and will be strengthened by eventual economic recovery. We need to plan for them, not least to avoid being propelled along by a series of such shocks.

Of course we are dealing with forces which are outside the Government's control. Essentially they are outside even global institutions' control because they are, at root, external constraints imposed by our planetary systems and resources.

So is it remotely fair for people to hold the Government responsible?

I think, sadly, it is. There may be a lot of people who are in denial and are helped to stay there by the media's disposition to blame the Government. That is the nature of this phase of the political cycle. But most people can understand the nature of the challenge: if there is lasting electoral anger over the impact of rising commodity costs, the root of it is the lack of preparation. Part of the job of the Government is effective planning to meet foreseeable strategic problems. Instead what the electorate has seen is a scramble to respond in a hurry. Our politics – right across the spectrum – is ill-adapted to engage with what we now need to contemplate, and people know it.

What faces us is nothing less than a realignment of politics, here and elsewhere. We are in trouble with our place on the planet and many of our current assumptions and behaviours are simply not relevant to this challenge. This pamphlet examines some of the main lines that would have to emerge in the journey to an ecologically intelligent politics.

Some of these changes look very challenging. Indeed, what has fuelled the growth of a minority independent green politics has been the perception that the dominant party ideologies are not capable of making them. This has been a rational position to take while those dominant ideologies have found themselves able to develop within the established social/economic framework of politics. But that framework cannot now survive for much longer without accommodating, at a fundamental level, the realities of human ecology. The independent green political project then begins to look very dated.

I do not know how this realignment will work out. It is a reasonable bet that, by the end of this century, the party lines of today – yes, even New Labour's – will look as quaint as the Whigs do to us. On the other hand, as I will argue, the fundamental instincts and strengths of the

Labour movement – equality, the priority given to the common interest, internationalism – could make it the most promising existing vehicle for this new politics.

Last year David Miliband, in his Fabian lecture, said this:

> "History gives us a warning. 100 years ago we had a dynamic social movement, led by trade unions, struggling to find a political home. Many within the labour movement, including Keir Hardie, began their life as Liberals. But the failure of the Liberal Party to open itself up to new ideas, to a new movement resulted in the creation of the Labour Party, the end of the liberals as a party of government, and a fatal division between progressives.

> Today, there are parallels with the environmental movement. It is a growing force in civil society, searching for a home in mainstream politics. The party that succeeds will be the natural party of government. At the next election, environmental credibility will be a threshold issue, alongside national security, economic policy and public service investment. Flunk on any of these and you are unelectable."

That is certainly true. I maintain that it goes beyond recruiting green votes into some sort of red-green alliance, which is how the speech was generally interpreted. We are not in the mergers and acquisitions business, and there are many aspects of current green politics – especially its attitude to science – that are dangerously irrelevant.

But the comparison with the early twentieth century is apt. Then a social movement found a vehicle – the Labour Party – relevant to the needs of the time. Over the rest of the century what started as a political struggle between the two seemingly intractable interests of labour and capital resulted in a synthesis which forms the basis of all politics today. Now we stand before a new imperative; that of creating a politics which meets our ecological as well as our social and economic needs. If we succeed in this, we can be sure that the resulting electoral politics will be as different from those of today as today's are from those of Edwardian Britain.

Anticipating those changes is made more difficult than necessary by the inadequacy of our current economic models. And because economics is now the pre-eminent discipline for making policy, I will start there. There is, of course, another reason to do so, because the problem is at heart an economic one. It's just that it's Nature's economics and not ours.

The Green Crunch

2. Towards an ecological economics

The first lesson of economics is scarcity: there is never enough of anything to satisfy all those who want it. The first lesson of politics is to disregard the first lesson of economics.
 – Thomas Sowell

L et's start with the problem. As it is an ecological one, let it be expressed by an ecologist, Janine Benyus: "We are ... beholden to ecological laws, the same as any other life form. The most irrevocable of these laws says that a species cannot occupy a niche that appropriates all resources... any species that ignores this law winds up destroying its own community to support its own expansion."[2]

We are in trouble with our place on the planet because we have easily exceeded the natural resource limits that Ms Benyus is talking about. We have been in trouble for some time, but now we are beginning to notice. Campaigns such as WWF's very effective 'One Planet Living' have brought this fact into much sharper focus, giving real public edge to what the science has been telling us.[3] The idea of environmental footprint – the impact that we have on natural systems and natural assets – is now common enough currency for car manufacturers to misuse it in their advertising.

This increasing familiarity is welcome but it has also bred a degree of complacency, a feeling that we don't really have to put ourselves out much to manage our way out of the problem, if there is one. Nothing could be more ill-judged in the face of the facts, and every senior politician who has had to deal with the facts ends up being gravely worried by them, but also faces a huge gap between the reality of the necessary responses and the electorate's readiness to accept them. As a result, the active management of our ecological niche is not something that has often troubled our politics, electoral or otherwise.

But now it has to; and that means principally that it must be brought alongside our economic thinking. The inescapable truth is that our economy relies on the physical and biological systems of the biosphere.

For economics and politics this hasn't so much mattered until quite recently. . We began as a small population in a large world and we could effectively treat global natural resources as infinite. The land might degrade so that our crops failed, the wood for our fires might run out; so we would move and start again elsewhere. Later in our history, our air and water might become dangerously loaded with pollution, so we would regulate the sources and clean them up. We have learnt to believe that these things can be managed with essentially local or national responses – it is only in the last 30 years that we have seen a few faltering attempts to adopt global remedies.

So the fact is that local economies have always been limited by local ecological constraints. But now something new has happened. In the last couple of generations our global economy is becoming limited by global ecological constraints such as climate impact. Because of this, we cannot necessarily rely on thinking that served us well in the past being adequate for the present challenge.

In particular, classical economics doesn't deal well with these global constraints. For most of its 200 year history it has effectively been assumed that what environmental scientists call sources and sinks are to all intents and purposes infinite. That is to say that the ability of our planet to provide resources and to absorb the deleterious impacts of human activity can be taken for granted, although there are costs attached to both processes which then do become the stuff of economics.

So what? To observe that classical economics doesn't provide an adequate analysis of the ecological challenge is neither particularly new nor does it devalue the usefulness of economics in its own field. Surely we can just keep the science and the dismal science separate? That would be fine but for two things: first, the fundamental interconnections that exist between the economy of nature – the flow of resources in the natural world and the state of the natural systems – and the economy of human activities.

Secondly, there is the compelling reality that all political classes now rely on economics as their touchstone for evaluating and making policy. I can see no prospect of our being able to inform decision-making in a crowded world without an economic policy rooted in physical & biological science. The development of the analytical tools and economic theory to support such a policy, has to be an urgent priority for government.

Think of this interface between the worlds of the natural and human economies as the border post of a country whose currency is not internationally traded. On the outside you can assemble a wealth of knowledge about natural systems, their interdependencies on each other and with humanity. By definition these are not all expressible in the same currency; nature is complex. But to bring those transactions into the country of classical economics you have to visit the *bureau de change* and turn them all into dollars. This may or may not make much sense. You have to haggle with the cashier over the exchange rates for the various denominations you are carrying. Even if you can agree on values, the important qualitative differences between the various goods – water, raw materials, energy, soils, ecosystems – all get lost as the values are homogenised by the conversion. You will probably decide that some of your denominations simply can't be converted in this way and you will leave them at the border, in which case they will play little part in any subsequent analysis. This is what has happened in real political life with certain ecological assets. We have international agreements which essentially treat certain species or sites as being non-tradeable, and for good reason, but it takes ecology to the margins of decision-making, waiting at the border of economic policy to hear its fate.

Of course it is right to try to allocate monetary values to ecological assets. That is, after all, what the Stern report has attempted for carbon mitigation costs. It is necessary to do so, even if it is not sufficient. In fact in the short to medium term it is a vital necessity and nothing that I will have to say about the need to develop a more comprehensive fusion of economic and ecological science should cloud the importance of doing valuation thoroughly and well.

I wrote earlier that we are now, for the first time, in the position where environmental constraints set limits to our existing economic activity. It is rational to respond to those constraints by trying to work out how to incorporate natural resource calculations into our mainstream economic models. Indeed that is what the growing discipline of environmental economics is about. Let me quote the guru of the field, the economist Herman Daly.[4]

"Economic logic remains the same; but the pattern of scarcity in the world changes, with the result that behaviour must change if it is to remain economic. Instead of maximising returns to and investing in man-made capital (as was appropriate in an empty world), we must now maximise returns to and invest in natural capital (as is appropriate in a full world). This is not 'new economics' but new behaviour consistent with old economics in a world with a new pattern of scarcities."

I can't say that I agree that there is no new economics – the sort of economics advocated by Professor Daly looks pretty new to me – but that is not the point. The point is that we have to broaden the scope of our economic thinking, and fast. One conclusion is that while we are doing this – and it will take time – our current economic policy has to be made to incentivise natural resource efficiency very strongly. Indeed this seems to me the absolute central principle for our medium-term economic policy if we are really interested in climbing out of the hole we

14

are still digging for ourselves in our pursuit of economic growth measured in monetary terms; and, boy, do we need to get out of that hole. That, of course, is where politics comes in.

Taking the political temperature

How seriously is politics taking the ecological challenge in the first decade of the 21st century?

Certainly there has been a very rapid shift, both on the right and left, in the number and salience of initiatives which respond in various ways to perceived environmental pressures, notably in the area of carbon policy. Variable road fund excise duty; congestion charging (admittedly not designed to limit carbon emissions); carbon trading; the extent of the obligations on energy companies to pay for domestic energy efficiency; the renewables obligation; and the insistence that by 2016, all new homes will be 'zero-carbon'. These would all have been practically inconceivable only 20 years ago.

There is, then, rapid movement in some areas. What has hardly shifted is the central core of policy (and that is most true of economic policy), and the core of electoral politics. I will stay with the issue of carbon policy, which was only just coming onto the political radar ten years ago, to explain why I say this.

The body politic appears to have agreed that atmospheric greenhouse gas concentrations are an important target for public policy, but in fact the actions still lag the rhetoric and, worse, are badly out of touch with the reality.

It's now a couple of years since the Competition Commissioner, Günter Verheugen, not a notable green, said "If something is ecologically wrong it can't be economically right" which just about says it all. The key EU economic platform, the Lisbon strategy, makes explicit reference to the opportunities presented by pursuing greater resource efficiency. But in reality the dynamic of the Lisbon Agenda is short-term rather than long-term competitiveness; for example the German government (Verheugen is a German Commissioner) has been busy lobbying against tighter vehicle emission standards on behalf of its big-car manufacturers.

Here in the UK, Tony Blair was genuinely seized by the issue of atmospheric carbon concentration – partly as a result, he said, of being nagged by his children when he first became Prime Minister. He made numerous statements about a specific form of resource efficiency, low-carbon energy, as part of his undoubted commitment to climate policy. Yet progress is much slower than hoped, and a series of genuinely tough decisions awaits in Energy policy. The UK still derives only about two per cent of its total energy needs from renewables.

Exhortation isn't enough. The dominant economic structures and assumptions actually militate against good intentions, however forcefully expressed. For example, after the Prime Minister had challenged UK business to do better on Climate Change in September 2004, he got a response from 13 Chief Executive Officers of major international companies offering a new partnership with Government but also observing that:

> "The private sector and governments are caught in a 'Catch-22' situation with regard to tackling climate change. Governments tend to feel limited in their ability to introduce new policies for reducing emissions because they fear business resistance, while companies are unable to take their investments in low-carbon solutions to scale because of lack of long-term policies."

This is as accurate a diagnosis today as it was four years ago. In particular, a reliable long-term carbon price signal is essential. Large investments being made today require at least some idea of the likely carbon price in the middle of the next decade, for example in large-scale power generation. As this (and it is not the same thing as the market price for oil or coal, but a creation of government through regulation) depends both on present policy and future politics, neither of which are exactly racing certainties, it is hardly surprising that industry feels that it does not have the long-term framework it craves.

Those CEOs hit the nail on the head, but sadly their far-sightedness is not typical of business as a whole. The interventions needed to shape our economy to adapt successfully to ecological constraint are almost universally resisted.

In this regard as in others the business lobbies, which wield immense influence at the centre of government, are rooted in the economic consensus of twenty years ago, that regulatory interventions are always an economic bad, economic instruments are always more efficient and that there are no profits, at the level of the firm or of the economy, in environmental performance.

But that thinking is dangerously out of date.[5] In fact, within mainstream economics there is now a body of work that recognises that future competitiveness will depend on high resource efficiency. This is a position put forward, for instance, by the Aldersgate Group.[6] In fact the idea that it is a good and strategic thing to secure our future competitiveness by going hard for a big improvement in resource efficiency now is so rarely contested that it deserves the Jane Austen tag – it is a truth universally acknowledged. But in practice it is never quite the right time to start because there are often costs in the short-term, we postpone doing anything very much until the market turns the corner, or we have seen off the competition from Eastern Europe, or the credit squeeze is over. More Augustine than Austen: *Lord, give me chastity and continence, but not yet*.

Even though there is some recognition of the fact that we are now draining our natural capital, the reality of day-to-day politics shows that that fact is not taken seriously. If we look at the current state of play we can see a number of significant examples of this.

Firstly, the UK environmental agenda is routinely seen as a regulatory 'burden'. The Government responds to business and political pressure with reviews (such as the Hampton Review), establishes the Better Regulation Executive which is then edged into deregulation, and brings out new legislation. The RES (Regulatory Enforcement and Sanctions) bill, which went through Parliament earlier this year (2008), was presented quite bluntly as a deregulatory measure when the minister, Lord Jones, introduced it in the Lords, and hardly any parliamentarians spoke in support of the bill's provisions for new penalties for enforcement.[7]

Secondly, starting roughly with Labour's second term, burgeoning social expenditure has begun to squeeze other spending with the result that Government, regardless of party, is bound to be increasingly risk averse to anything which might be seen to reduce short term economic growth and tax revenues.

Third, the combination of the credit crunch and the rise in commodity prices makes governments of any stripe unwilling to carry through any policy on resource consumption which relies on a price signal. It also becomes helpless in the face of rising commodity prices precisely because it has not prepared itself or the electorate for the end of the era of artificially cheap resources.

Fourthly, the EU is also concerned about low growth, and in face of Asian competition and increasing social burden (in the cost of pensions for example) questions the affordability of EU environmental standards. It is also ready to allow large exemptions from, say, carbon caps to protect sectors of its industry most at risk from a combination of competition and high carbon input, rather than use the opportunity for technology forcing to gain greater future competitiveness.

None of this should be surprising but it should be sobering. The inertia involved in now changing our politics is immense. Scientific analysis of the likely pace and scale of climate change has to make estimates of the speed of response of huge geophysical systems – the oceans, the ice-sheets and so on. Just as important a factor in our calculations should be an appreciation of the speed of response of the political environment, and nobody can believe that the politics and institutions of a world that is managing itself sustainably are going to arise in short order. This will be a generational change – which is one good reason why it is wise to begin to plan for adapting to some inevitable long-term climate change.

But we start in a dangerous place, because politics in the democratic world over the last 70 years has equated success with economic growth as we currently define it. Any personal economic detriment is deemed to signal political failure. The long journey away from the gods of consumption has to be begun soon.

The most obvious manifestation of this danger is that government does not have the context of principles – what we have learnt since 1997 to call the 'narrative' – to sustain positions which attempt to allocate the correct costs to resources.

There are formidable electoral obstacles to this. In the carbon realm, rising fuel costs and the resultant general inflation on core shopping basket goods will quite simply see you out of office. Once in office, you will be keen to limit carbon emissions but just not able to contemplate the necessary actions – for instance in the field of transport – because of the anticipated electoral response. And that's not because the electorate doesn't know that there is a problem – in fact I think people would quite like someone to square with them about it – and only partly because it is in denial. It's because there isn't yet a convincing set of remedies being offered.

When it comes to politics, Bill Clinton summarised our position in three words: "the economy, stupid". This doesn't just apply to the West. In the developing economies the pressure for cheap consumption is if anything, and understandably, greater.

But when it comes to our fate as a species and our long-term well being as individuals, it isn't the economy: it's the ecology, stupid. So we do need, in the long term, a new way of doing economics. And we need a transition strategy to get us from where we are to where we need to be.

New directions

There may as yet be no coherent political strategy but that doesn't mean that nothing has been done. Any government at any time has to deal with the issues of the day and the facts of contemporary social and economic life even when those issues do not figure boldly in party manifestos or election campaigns. This is how it has been in the last decade or so with the interplay of economic and environmental forces (I am studiously trying to avoid abuse of the term 'sustainable development' here).

For someone like me, who has observed the development of environmental policy for at least the last quarter of a century, the speed with which we have seen new initiatives taken by government has been very welcome, and nowhere is this more true than in the UK. Taking the 1992 Earth summit as a convenient and significant starting point, domestic policy under both the Major and Blair governments has moved much more positively than we might have thought, and the Labour Government since 1997 can justifiably claim much credit. From relatively minor changes like variable Vehicle Excise Duty to far-reaching ones like the establishment of a regulated market in industrial carbon allocations (which added another string to the bow of the City of London's pre-eminence in European markets), many of the initiatives being advocated in the 90's have found their way into policy. The UK has played an important part in promoting international agreements such as Kyoto and it is significant that politicians from all parties are impatient for faster progress on global action.

We therefore have some grounds for optimism; but we must also look squarely at some other, less encouraging, features of this period. The most striking to me is the fact that most of these advances have been made by the political classes, often with cross-party agreement, but with very little exposure to the will of the electorate.

As seen from Westminster, the picture is one of conclusive science, emerging international pressures, a growing problem which has to be dealt with. But the public perception, even of human-induced climate

20

change, is far less coherent. Surveys of media coverage still show a surprising parity between material supporting the reality of climate change and material denying it, or at least its human-induced component. To put it simply, the Government Chief Scientist may have the ear of the decision-makers but Jeremy Clarkson has the ear of the electorate.

As a result, the good initiatives tend to be unconnected bits of policy, brought in as opportunity permits but without a unifying political strategy. When the going gets really tough, as with the fuel protests, political resolve weakens, not only in Westminster; even the voices of the green NGOs were strangely subdued in the face of public anxiety over being able to get petrol. Gordon Brown's first budget was accompanied by a Green Fiscal policy document which explicitly recognised the potential for using tax incentives as part of an environmental policy kit and not simply for revenue raising – by definition most environmental taxes erase themselves exactly in proportion to their success in changing behaviours. Yet in ten years, and with a couple of creditable exceptions like the landfill tax escalator, there has been very little actual use of the tax system in the way the document promised.

The truth is that green policy has remained largely marginal to the centre of Government, a marginalisation reinforced both by the political naivety of some of its proponents and by the myopic world view of the community of core economic and political advisors.[8] Proof of this, if proof were needed, has been the way in which election manifestos have treated the subject. It's there, but it is not a core part of the political brand of either party that thinks it might get elected. And so carbon policy, for instance, develops almost as a branch of administration, in a political no-man's-land, depending on the support of the elite rather than drawing strength from electoral demand, unable to develop beyond where the elite is prepared to allow it to go.

The gap in understanding between the centre and the public has stretched the political elastic just about as far as it can go, and the time is now long overdue for the gap to be filled by some determined political leadership.

I have just complained that green policy remains largely marginal but there has been one recent counter-example: the Stern report.[9] The real significance of Stern is that it forces the issue onto the core economic agenda, so it is worth reflecting on what that may mean.

Lord Stern's approach is foursquare within the valuation approach which I described earlier. When confronted with the incompatibility of human economic activity with the economy of Nature, the first rational response is to use the economic systems we are familiar with and to bring in values and costs for ecological resources or sinks.

In calculating the costs of current action to alleviate future climate impacts and comparing them with the costs of future adaptation, Stern put the science under the nose of the economists for the first time. The report met with a chorus of approval (including from me) because it was a senior economist getting serious about applying his discipline to the most pressing of the current threats caused by our outgrowing our place in the planet.

Politicians sat up and took notice in a way that they had not when there were no dollar signs attached to the problem. Or, to be accurate, there were, but they hadn't been put there by the priesthood of the economy.

Now I would bet that the Stern estimates turn out wide of the mark, both underestimating the costs of mitigation and of failure to mitigate, not least because there are other ecological constraints to the continued growth that he projects into the future. And in fact over the summer Nick Stern has come out revising his cost estimate upwards.

But whether or not you believe the estimates, his report is important because it legitimises actions at a strategic, macro level, which will become part of the core agenda for political leaders in this century. And in order to do that he had to step outside the normal disciplines of economic valuation by using a very low discount rate, essentially according the future costs of climate adaptation a much higher current value than is usual. Had he not done so, the net present value of even the most drastic future adjustments would have

22

melted into insignificance. Nothing could more clearly illustrate the difficulty of using classical economic analysis to deal with long-term strategy.

The political impact of accepting Stern's analysis is considerable and as yet not well appreciated. Among other things, we will see carbon costing develop, the resultant price signals will inform both public and private sector decision-making and a genuine public politics, deeper than the current bar-room chat about climate and broader than the rather dry, technical nature of current policy making, will have to follow.

This is all welcome but it isn't enough to deal with the challenge. Price by itself, unless it is set eye-wateringly high, cannot deliver the long-term goal of 80 per cent decarbonisation just declared by the embryonic Committee on Climate Change, nor indeed is 80 per cent certain to be enough in the light of the most recent scientific assessment. The market alone cannot be relied on and it is clear that there has also to be a regulatory response, so that policy will have to manage carbon targets directly as well as managing their monetisation within the money economy.

But can we call climate change the 'greatest market failure'? No. There are others, which I don't see any hope of bringing to light in the same way using our current economic models.

Can we see how to answer the simple question "How much wild does a world of nine billion human beings need?"[10] Can we answer it in a way that will be really useful for policy making?

Can we answer a question which is nearly unapproachable in a free society: "What lifestyle do we aspire to in the long run, and what global population does that support?"

These questions are simple enough to state but beyond the scope of monetary economics, and we shouldn't ask it to address them unaided. Most questions within the economics of Nature are like this. In many ways carbon is a bad example, because it is easily quantified, the effects we are principally concerned to manage are physical ones, the carbon cycle is relatively well understood, and it already has a significant role in our human economies. Even so, as we have just seen, its management requires a kind of twin-track approach. Other ecological constraints are much less accessible, especially those based on biological stocks and flows.

Faced with the economics of Nature, our current economic models aren't getting us anywhere much. We are retrofitting them with regulatory prohibitions of doubtful enforcement, market interventions of limited scope, product information which most consumers don't notice. This is not the way to enable political leaders to deal with humanity's most pressing physical issue.

And I'm not just talking about the big macro-economic choices.

Because we don't yet have the right political context, smaller decisions are also more difficult than we can afford them to be. The upcoming decision on the Severn Barrage is an instructive case in point. I think it is obvious that the key consideration for the decision-makers will be the energy economics, although there is also sharp political pressure arising from our European undertaking on the renewables target. It will be hard enough to get the energy cost-benefit calculations right but the future cost of carbon makes this proposal much more likely to be agreed in contrast to previous attempts.

But how do we deal with the other issues? In particular, how do we deal with the eco-system impacts? In today's world, the valuation methodologies rest on rather thin foundations. I have just seen a major analysis of energy policy which makes the argument that the present ecology of the Severn estuary is rather sparse – it is a hostile, tide-scoured environment – and that the conditions for life in habitats modified by a tidal barrage will be more productive.[11] This is true, of course. The sheer tonnage of biomass would be much greater in a less aggressive, managed environment. The range of species is also likely to be greater. But both of these facts miss one of the main points about biodiversity which is that the score is kept globally as well as locally and global biodiversity is always damaged by the loss of a scarce habitat –

the very starkness of the place and the rarity of its conditions are what can make it important. It is, however, nearly impossible to bring a valuation based on global significance into any sensible and proportionate analysis of what are otherwise at most national costs and benefits.

Here we come up against one of the most obvious features of environmental economics; the limited tradeability of ecological assets. Essentially there are two approaches in the short history of environmental economics, which has largely concerned itself with determining what value to place upon natural assets when we are considering the case or the costs for their protection: you can look for the right way of according something its economic value and then decide if it can be traded for some other good, or you can treat it as essentially of infinite value and protect it literally at all costs. I won't detain you with a discussion of the philosophical divide that yawns here because in practice, both approaches are used in different ways in policy. We do subject a wide range of proposals to Strategic Environmental Assessment, which usually entails some sort of cost/benefit calculation on the conservation elements; and we also aim to give certain species and sites absolute protection.

What I want to point out is that the game is changing. In this century we are no longer thinking simply about environmental protection. We want to manage the flows of natural resources through our human economies and societies and husband their stocks. This clearly cannot be done solely by attaching monetary values to these assets, and effectively treating them as wholly tradable, nor solely by according some of them infinite value so they cannot be traded at all. Instead we need to identify the key natural resources that need to be actively managed and pursue a multivariate resource economics – by which I mean optimising economic policy against a basket of resource measures – which is what may happen *de facto* with carbon, providing that the control total is derived from science and not from political considerations. For sensible political choices to be made, however, we need much better and more reliable measures; and not just of physical resources, but crucially of biological ones as well.

Going back to the Severn Barrage decision, we can see that the argument will be about the non-tradeable assets and therefore about legal and treaty obligations – the Habitats and Birds Directives of the EU – and whether they can be circumvented or somehow managed. Treaty obligations which exist precisely because we have taken the view that certain natural assets, not expressible in monetary terms, should be essentially outside the realm of monetary negotiation.

This is wise in our current circumstances but too limited to be an intelligent and systematic way of making decisions about our management of our niche. It also succeeds in setting economic and ecological arguments against each other, and therefore makes their proponents less likely to value each other's insights; surely the most stupid position to take given the nature of our predicament.

We need – and quickly – a fusion of the disciplines. The transactions and flows of the economy take place within the real world of human ecology and its flows of resource which are partly created, largely mediated by life itself, by the biosphere.

Presenting economic decisions outside of this context is now inadequate. The challenge to both economists and ecologists is to develop models of thinking about human activity which embed economic analysis within a realistic understanding of the natural systems on which the economy is constructed.

3. The political challenges in practice

So far, this argument has been an appeal for the rapid development of a more effective economic-scientific theory in order to support political decision-making. It has been an appeal for overdue political leadership and for a coherent strategy.

This section looks at the issues that such a strategy will have to deal with and what they mean for Labour, both by way of problems and opportunities.

I am not going to start with a set of general principles. If we already had an available ideology which allowed us to deal confidently with these matters I wouldn't be writing this and you wouldn't want to read it if I did. I am going to deal with a number of current policy areas which are all obviously connected to the problem of managing our ecological status. It will quickly be evident that these areas are as likely to be in social policy or in our cultural and political assumptions as they are to be in the ecological and economic fields which have so far dominated this argument.

It will also quickly be evident that the problems thrown up by the impact of what I called 'the economics of Nature' are not merely technical. There are implications for our core values and for the relationship between the individual and the collective – in fact the three-way balance between individual, society, and the physical world – which go to the heart of political ideology.

This isn't difficult to see if we consider what might go wrong in the absence of what I called an ecological strategy.

It doesn't take too much imagination to envisage a series of severe resource shocks against an unprepared and weak global polity creating the conditions for chaotic and authoritarian responses. It might be an oil shock, but more dangerous would be a grain shock. This is not too fanciful an idea. Rising demand for grain and grain-fed protein, together with the diversion of a good proportion of the North American surplus into biofuel production – a surplus that has for decades kept the world grain markets stable and liquid – has already tightened the world grain market, pushed up prices, and had concomitant impacts on other commodity markets such as rice and soya. In 2008 some big rice exporters, notably India, have simply battened down the hatches and kept their rice at home.

It doesn't take too much imagination to wonder whether we can design what have, by definition, to be collective strategies in societies which have lost their instinct for collective action. Our collective intelligence finds its expression in many ways, but collective action depends quite crucially on the strength and effectiveness of our political institutions, whether that be the global control of atmospheric carbon through international agreements or the drive to get renewable energy infrastructure through national and local planning regimes. Can the requisite confidence in these institutions be made available in an atomised world?

It doesn't take too much imagination to think that even evidently effective long-term strategies might fail to win a democratic mandate. In fact that is exactly where we are today.

None of these imaginings is reason to give up on individual freedom, the benefits of regulated markets or democracy. But they are clues as to what the political questions are: the need for effective global institutions; national strategies which are taken out of the electoral cycle;

equity of access to natural resource; the fact that any form of large scale management of our natural resource flows entails significant intervention in the markets; and how we decouple aspiration from consumption in the democracies.

Resource pricing and availability

This winter of 2008-9 is likely to illustrate one of the most difficult problems arising from the end of the era of low commodity prices, and a problem that is especially difficult for Labour. Gas and electricity bills are rising rapidly in response to wholesale markets and to the price of oil. Those who will feel this most are the poor, but it will hurt a significant proportion of the electorate, compounding the problems of recession and job insecurity caused by the mayhem in the financial sector. The Government's response – targeting help to pensioners and at the longer-term protection represented by increased domestic energy efficiency – is sensible but is not likely to make most people feel that much better in the short term.

The difficulty is obvious. On the one hand, we are seeing an inevitable price correction which ought to help promote investment in both energy efficiency and alternatives to fossil fuels. If the price signal for carbon was what we wanted to use in order to create the conditions for a low-carbon economy, then the market is doing our job for us. But it is doing it in a way that is deeply regressive, inequitable and certain to increase fuel poverty. That's how liberalised markets tend to work.

It is extremely unlikely that we will ever get back to the retail energy prices of the last 15 years or so. Yet I do not think that this fact is being squarely presented to the electorate nor would it be an obvious vote-winner to do so. In fact the way in which we have communicated our political objectives during that period has predisposed the electorate to regard rising energy costs as a failure of politics. From gas privatisation onwards maintaining low prices has been part of the purpose of politics in the UK, even more than energy security. We have rejoiced, I fear rather too smugly, at our superiority over other European economies with their far less thoroughly liberalised energy markets. We have tasked the economic regulator, Ofgem, with one key objective: to keep prices low.[12]

Now we need to do two things that cut right across the grain of our recent history. Firstly, we need to acknowledge that there is, in a civilised society, a right to expect affordable access to warmth, light, and the other benefits which energy delivers and that this can only be protected as prices rise by intervention, either in the energy markets or through the welfare system. This awkward question has not troubled us much while energy prices have been low. Secondly, because carbon costs will need to be increased whatever the energy markets are doing, we have to force the pace of transition to non-carbon energy much more vigorously than at present. I'd like to say that it is an open question as to whether either of these goals can be achieved in the liberalised market set up in the 1980s; but that would mean that I had some reason to hope it to be possible.

There is not space to try to provide a comprehensive energy policy here. But I think we can derive some important clues if we think about the problem in the context of the principles of natural balance and the management of our ecological impact that I set out earlier.

The main strategic objectives are already defined.[13] Decarbonisation, especially of electricity generation, led by the carbon targets regime contained in the Climate Change Bill shortly to become law, and security of supply. That means that at some point in the foreseeable future we hope to have a mix of low or zero-carbon generation – which will inevitably include nuclear and may include an as yet unknown proportion of coal with carbon capture – dominating electricity production, and much wider use of local, on-site renewables which are likely to be significant, not so much for their aggregate contribution to overall energy flows but for the fact that they will require a more flexible and open grid system. In addition there must be much greater recovery and use of heat in the generating process, either local or national. This latter carries significant infrastructure costs and needs the sort of determined collective planning that seems so foreign to our present culture but which would have seemed natural enough 50 years ago. And on the demand side, our efficiency in the use of energy, whether domestic or commercial, will be much higher.

All this comes at a cost. It is obviously a very different regime. Not only will there be costs involved in the transition, the mix described above will result in a higher long-term unit price than in the past.

Present policy should therefore aim to do several things:

- to create the conditions for stability in the eventual long-term price; to minimise it so far as is consistent with stability;

- to consider its affordability and what interventions – welfare, subsidy, tariff regulation – are appropriate if the retail price is seen as unaffordable;

- to manage the evolution from current to future prices in a way that gives a high degree of predictability for both commercial invest-ment and domestic planning, and at a pace which is realistic;

- to plan the industrial transition so that investment and employ-ment are captured in the national economy and the benefits to national competitiveness are maximised.

These are hard arguments to make. To modern ears they sound statist. The mechanisms would certainly be ones which favour the collective interest: price control, presumably through regulation; social tariffs; an industrial strategy linking heavy public sector support for new tech-nologies to private investment planning; the use of the tax system to manage the price trajectory against a backdrop of fluctuating global wholesale markets, recycling a variable tax take into subsidy for indus-trial transition or social tariffs. These are all heavy interventions in an age which despises regulation; could we begin to contemplate them?

31

Well, yes. I say this because we already are. Lets look at them in turn. Price control? Social tariffs? The regulation of the water industry is already about 20 years old and it is both a price control mechanism, and an investment planning mechanism. For good measure it also looks a lot like a tax system, its income being based on the fossil remnants of a past property tax. All it lacks is a long-term price and investment strategy and the Government is now aiming to provide that too. And as the concerns about water resource management grow – for there are security of supply worries here too – and the real price of water escalates, we are seeing the rapid spread of metering which is planned to pave the way for social tariffs to protect the right of access to a vital natural resource. These constraints have co-existed with privatised water companies being merged, bought and sold, solid share prices (water company shares are famously reliable investments) and the world has not ground to a halt. Water and energy may not be the same thing but the similarities are striking; both are natural resources essential both to civilised life and to the economy. Both require a degree of ecological management. The main difference is that this has always been a recognised part of the water industry for the simple reason that the consequences of failing to manage Nature's economy in the water environment stare us in the face; rivers dry up or flood; crops fail; pollution makes people get ill.

Tax as a means of managing a price transition? What else is landfill tax? It even seems that Conservative policy has considered the possibilities of a counter-cyclical fiscal regime for stabilising energy price trends, so maybe the idea isn't that exotic. And in any event we *will* have a price transition because the market price of carbon is on an upward trend. Eventually, either through the operation of the usual market forces, or through regulation such as the EU emission trading regime, the price of carbon will rise to a point where substitute technologies become economic and are drawn into the market. This will take longer and be more uncertain, and therefore costly, in the absence of a planned approach.

An explicit industrial transition strategy? Well, yes, this does seem a long way off, though it is the one policy that everyone from the renewable lobbies to the Regional Development Agencies wants. One result of the Danes forcing the pace on windpower development by public subsidy or the Germans expanding their small-scale renewables by paying a reasonably attractive price for electricity fed into the grid, has been that we are now scrambling to buy the products of the industries that they created, and doing so in a seller's market. This summer the Government announced a massive expansion of offshore wind generation which will raise demand through the roof but there has been almost no forward planning on the supply side. As a result, other economies' order books are full and costs are escalating.

This theme of planning ahead is one that recurs over and over again in any address to resource management. But in the case of planning a rapid transition, heavily driven by the state, to a low-carbon energy economy, the remedy also benefits that other main strategic objective, energy security. As noted earlier, regardless of whether we have reached peak oil production, the rising world demand for fossil fuel has prices on an inexorable upward trend and is tightening the market. In these conditions prices around the rising trend will inevitably behave with greater volatility and control of resources will become as important as the market in determining where they are allocated – or grabbed might be a more accurate description. The sooner we loosen our dependence on such resources the better. It is extraordinary that only a few years ago energy economists were confident that domestic security of supply was a second-order problem, because the fundamental resource conditions that I have described were as evident then as now.[14] No-one today thinks that security of supply is a trivial issue, but our position has worsened because that period of inaction has cost us that completely non-renewable resource, time.

I do not think that Barack Obama won the US presidential election *because* of his energy policy, but he did win, in the gas-addicted USA, with an energy programme that used worries over oil security to mobilise support for a drive towards renewables and energy efficiency and at the same time the creation of new jobs.[15]

One of the consequences of having failed to deal quickly enough with systematic decarbonisation of energy production is that the pressure has risen on finding other ways of reducing our overall emissions. In the absence of readily available renewable substitutes, the important area of demand management has been joined by what are essentially rationing arguments. At one level that is, of course, what the EU trading system is – it sets a control total for the industries within the regime and lets the market in carbon allocations which this creates chase down the most efficient ways of delivering emission cuts. It is important, not so much for world carbon emissions, but for the speed of transition of Europe's industrial base, that this rationing works and that firms are not able to meet more than a small proportion of their cuts by buying them in world markets.[16] This form of rationing, setting a challenging but achievable target in order to drive technological improvement, makes sense.

What is more worrying is the interest that is being shown in personal carbon allowances. Personal rationing has never been popular and has always created a black market. Except in times of true national emergency, the only justification for any control system of this sort is to push people from one set of behaviours into another, which is justified by the collective good. Until there are alternative low-carbon behaviours and products available, personal carbon rationing would be an essentially authoritarian intervention. This is why we must start large-scale decarbonisation at the production end. But it also illustrates one of the ideological pitfalls for an ecological politics, which is its ability to proceed smoothly from the collective to the authoritarian, and why the social democratic left needs to offer a more liberal version of collective action.

The whole of this argument about resource pricing and availability has centred on the carbon resources in energy production; this is obviously sensible because it is a key area for current policy and its very topicality makes it an effective example. But similar arguments apply to the politics of managing any physical resource and some biological ones. Price, whether a market price or one created by regulation based, one supposes, on some monetary valuation of the resource, is not enough on its own. It has to be used alongside planning, in many cases quite heavy planning.[17]

I have already explained why this should be; but there is another quite practical reason which has been illustrated this year as the market oil price has escalated. The theory is that when the price of one resource gets too high (in this case the carbon in oil), other substitutes will come to market; and so they have. At some point on its way to $100 a barrel – my guess is at around $70 – it became economic for the oil companies to begin the serious exploitation of tar sands for oil extraction , a practice which is in fact worse from the point of view of carbon emissions as well as ecological damage.[18]

Demand management

Having opened the Pandora's box of carbon and energy policy to illustrate the nature of the industrial and supply policies which resource management calls into play, three other areas need to be mentioned which again are present in all resource politics: the global nature of the problem and therefore the need for global responses to be consistent; the steps we will need to take to deal with the existing impacts of the absence of effective policy in the past; and the subject of this section, demand management.

I have less to say here partly because current UK policy has made most progress in this area, or at least in beginning to address it. But in fact it is the most important part of resource politics. We must press hard on finding alternatives to carbon in our energy economy because the situation is truly serious; but we must not behave as if renewables are a free ride, and regrettably we usually do. People of my age may yet remember the 'electricity too cheap to meter' promised at the start of the nuclear power programme. Such dawns are always false ones. The wise management of natural resources in a crowded world requires an instinct for efficiency of use, not to say thrift.[19] Demand management matters.

We see this coming through strongly in Government policy towards the built environment, and this is rational given that the built environment is what accounts for about half of our carbon emissions. It also accounts for a high proportion of water use, and occupies an important position in the management of material resources, normally but now unhelpfully referred to as waste management.

New build in the UK has not had a great record on environmental efficiency, to say the least. Comparison with other northern European countries on such matters as energy standards is uncomfortable; we have bowed to an habitual industry lobby, against the costs of raising standards, with the result that we are now playing catch-up, and probably at greater cost. But the present Government has certainly confronted the issue; its commitment to zero-carbon for all new homes by 2016 is ambitious and just about achievable. The performance standards for the proposed eco-towns are encouraging. And the pace of change in building standards coupled with the introduction of the Code for Sustainable Homes gives an unmistakeable signal to the construction industry.[20] Public procurement has perhaps not kept up with these advances, and having set out its stall the Government has now to carry through its intentions in practice; but it has shown some determination to do so.

Dealing with the inefficiency of the existing building stock will be a more complex and extended process. Government after all has very few ways of intervening in the life of a building after it has been placed on the market. There has been a lot of recent policy activity here – especially in the realm of domestic energy efficiency, the impact of which will have to be closely monitored. Here is one area, however, where the rising retail cost of energy will bring forward much more private investment, especially if it accompanied by effective public incentives.

The activity and determination shown in demand policy for the built environment are harder to match elsewhere, particularly in transport, where the politics and the means of implementation are both more difficult, and decarbonisation is in its infancy. A full discussion of transport policy is not possible here. I simply want to record that in any future scenario of a sustainable society, public transport plays a significant role, and it is the planning and financial implications which will particularly matter.

And in fact transport is one of the many issues for which Government policy matters, but local practice matters just as much. Having been Leader of a large Metropolitan Council for over a decade, I am anxious to emphasise the contribution of local government to sustainable resource management. Urban policy is an indispensable part of the management of our place on the planet.

I say this for strategic as well as practical reasons. Only recently, in this decade, humanity passed a significant tipping point when for the first time more than 50 per cent of the Earth's human population lives in cities. We are increasingly an urban animal. How our cities function as environmental communities is therefore important, and not only by virtue of population. For it is in the organisation of urban life – its transport patterns, its demands on energy, water, food, materials etc – that the real opportunity lies for finding ways of reducing our average impact on nature. If the city can become successful in ecological terms, we will have won the battle.

Urban management has therefore to be an important part of any politics of sustainability. There are formidable obstacles to this, the most obvious being that, by virtue of the fact that city life is removed from most of the obvious stimuli that would awaken an understanding of the importance of natural balance, the practice of urban politics and the preoccupations of urban populations have almost wholly ignored the issues.

This is why it is more than a local issue. The framework for urban policy must be structured so as to call forth more appropriate responses.

Fortunately some of this can be done by developing the idea of the environmental footprint of cities, as introduced recently by WWF into a more hard-headed and quantifiable set of resource efficiency indicators.

Rather harder but still eventually necessary will be the development of a much deeper understanding of how cities work in and with their hinterland, which will also help to overcome some of the very unnecessary divide between urban and rural interests and politics that currently gets in the way. Along the way we should see whether the cities can be given more control over their own infrastructure; after all, the history of most of the public utilities begins in municipal effort. The fact is that mayors and city leaders have not had to think much about where the water or power comes from since these resource flows were provided by the state and then private utilities. Even those that did found it hard to get any data. In my time as a council leader you couldn't find out what quantity of electricity was being consumed in any given area, because although the supply companies had the data they regarded it as a commercial secret which they were not prepared to divulge even to the state.

Before leaving this short review of demand management I should touch on the issue of the flow of material resources through our economy and society. It seems to me to be very likely that we will, in the next decade, see a real shift from waste management to genuine resource management, with the recovery and re-use of a high percentage of the vast industrial, commercial and construction material flows; this has been pump-primed by the landfill tax escalator, an excellent if at first rather hesitant example of how to use the levers of government to anticipate and shape the future, but it will be driven more by rising material costs and world demand. Already large quantities of used resource – paper, plastic, metals – are shipped from the UK to the resource-hungry economies of China and India. This pressure will weaken during recession but will return with recovery.

The same economic forces are beginning to drive serious demand reduction in industry. Various claims have been made by academics and campaigners about the need to dematerialise production by sharply increasing resource efficiency by 'factor 4' or 'factor 10'.[21] Whatever the factor, industry will have to improve its performance in response to input costs. The issue for economic policy is that, in addition to the short term need to avoid cost, there is a long-term competitive advantage to be gained for the UK by anticipating the future and making the investment to gain step-change rather than incremental improvement as early as possible. This was an important theme for the Commission on Environmental Markets and Economic Performance (CEMEP), set up by Gordon Brown in the wake of the Stern report, with two Secretaries of State co-chairing it.[22] Yet I have difficulty detecting much enthusiasm for getting to grips with this aspect of industrial strategy; just as was noted earlier in respect of the lead that we have conceded to other economies in wind energy, we don't seem to want to force the pace or the direction of industrial development.

Pace and adaptation

It can sometimes seem as if the problem of the large-scale management of natural resources has crept up on us. It hasn't, of course. The natural species optimism – a necessary feature of our evolutionary progress – has helped us to turn Nelson's eye to the evidence over quite a long period, on the grounds that we always find some way of overcoming or at least riding the forces of Nature; we always have so far. We shouldn't decry this optimism but we should understand that it is at play, especially in the arguments for the so-called 'techno-fix'. This is the belief that technological advance will always allow us to meet both escalating population and per capita demand, and it is routinely brought into the debate about resources from energy to food production. One of its current manifestations is in the belief, which may turn out to be correct but cannot be taken as certain, that carbon capture and storage will be capable of being used on a large scale to decarbonise the generation of electricity from coal; another is the conviction that improved agricultural methods and the bringing into production of new tracts of land will keep pace with the projected growth of population plus higher nutritional demand.

There is no more justification for dismissing these claims than there is for accepting them. We need be neither extreme optimists nor extreme pessimists. But we do need to deal with the world as we find it, or as we can rationally expect it to be in the foreseeable future. And the fact is that technology has kept up with some of the natural pressures. Some, but not all.

The first consequence of this is that many of our responses now require much more pace than is usually found in political processes. The previous pages carry many examples of this, such as the zero-carbon homes target. In particular, carbon mitigation policy is replete with examples of actions which we know are necessary, where some sort of political agreement, even explicit policy target, has been reached, and yet where our ability to carry that through to implementation in the relevant timescale is questionable.

There is a sense of rush, of hurry, about the whole enterprise. The UK is to set up a statutory committee with the express purpose of defining targets and timescales for decarbonisation, and then of holding Government to account for their achievement.[23] This is a far-sighted, brave and significant initiative, the first of its kind in the democratic world. But who can doubt that this committee will spend much of its time exhorting the Government of the day to greater and more urgent efforts? Its very existence is born of urgency. Urgency which is driven by what we know now to be necessary, and which is increased every time that a new scientific assessment is made; for the scientists have been cautious, conservative, even perhaps optimistic in their advice, and most politicians have not surprisingly interpreted this as lack of certainty.[24]

So far, this need for pace has not been met. Democratic politics rarely mobilises suddenly, and this is mostly a very good thing. But a weakness of our present situation is that, as pointed out before, the electoral demand for change is frail and unformed, and lacks political leadership around which to condense. So change has been pursued tentatively. This is why environmental campaigners and advocates increasingly resort to the language of war; because it feels as if we need to acknowledge an urgency amounting to emergency, which will provide the spur for action.

The second consequence of past inaction is the need to begin a serious strategy of adapting our economy and society to the inevitable impacts of existing changes that we have wrought in natural systems, and the most obvious and most urgent of these is adaptation to climate change. Over the last year, while the Climate Change Bill has been in draft and then in Parliament, all eyes have been on mitigation policy. The Bill as originally drafted made no statutory provision for adaptation along the lines being proposed for mitigation, and it took a considerable effort to get included some basic powers for government to monitor and direct the capacity of the nation to cope with climate impacts.

Climate adaptation is coming up fast on the rails. This encompasses a series of issues, most of which are very practical, as the summer floods of 2007 demonstrated in dramatic fashion. Drinking water supplies were interrupted over a sizeable area, and the army was called in to help with emergency water distribution, because of the flooding of a key water treatment works at Mythe near Gloucester. In the same part of the country an electricity substation which was a key node in the grid was only just saved from being knocked out by floodwater by the determined efforts of emergency workers to erect temporary barriers in dangerous conditions. Had they not succeeded several hundred thousand people and some infrastructure of regional and national importance would have been without mains electricity for weeks. In South Yorkshire there was grave concern over the stability of the dam wall of a smallish reservoir, which had to be drained down. The M1 – in the direct line of the flow-path had the dam failed – was closed, and Sheffield's power supply threatened. In Hull the urban drainage system – not its flood defences – was overwhelmed by concentrated heavy rain with the result that as

41

many properties were flooded in the city as in the whole of the rest of the country put together.

This series of events underlines just how vulnerable some of our national infrastructure is to climate impacts. In some respects we were lucky – we escaped the social chaos that would follow a prolonged loss of power for a large urban area – but we escaped it by the skin of our teeth. Government acted quickly after the floods had subsided to begin to assess the risk to infrastructure, but it will be a long job. Road, rail, power, water, communications, emergency services, hospitals, schools, care homes – you name it, it has vulnerabilities. From my experience with the Environment Agency I can find examples of each of these being knocked out in flooding.

Building the resilience of our infrastructure is therefore one of the adaptation issues, but there are others. In the face of rising sea level and increased risk from tidal surges, the question of what constitutes a sustainable and defensible coastline is one that will loom ever larger in the coming period, especially but not only in the East of England. Among these concerns will be the ongoing management of the tidal regime in the Thames estuary, where the barrier and its associated downstream defence systems were built in the wake of the 1953 tidal surge which killed over 300 people in England and many more in the Netherlands. Today those defences still offer a high but declining level of security to 1.25 million people and nearly £100bn worth of assets in the London floodplain.

Climate forecasts currently look at what might happen under a range of political and economic scenarios. In all the most likely scenarios, the strong probability is that in the 21st century this country will experience wetter winters, and hotter, drier summers, but that in these generally hotter summers there will be an increasing frequency of extreme rainfall events.[25] It must be immediately evident then, that there are other things than flood risk to consider when we are thinking about how we will adapt. For example, agricultural patterns and practices will alter, though this is an area where policy may not have to intervene to do more than shape and enable natural changes.[26]

The other big issue will be heat. Most British people joke that a bit of global warming would be a good idea; some of them also believe it. But the point of thinking about adaptation is to prepare for, not to bemoan, change, and a hotter summer climate will mean quite deep changes to design of buildings, of urban areas, to how we live; and some of these need to be thought about now. And increased summer heat also has a more brutal edge; in the European heat wave of 2003, there were widespread water shortages, crop failure, and between 30,000 and 40,000 deaths advanced by the effects of heat. It was a record summer; the August heat 'anomaly', as it was expressed by the meteorologists, was 3°C – that is 3°C above the average temperature across most of the continent. The climate forecasts suggest quite strongly that, by the middle of this century, this will not be an anomaly but a common occurrence. Before the end of the century, it will be an average summer.

Right at the beginning of this piece I described it as a call to embed an ecological understanding into our political principles and to accept that the management of our place in the natural world is as important a political purpose as economic or social management. But whether you agree with this statement or not, the preceding paragraphs must make it clear that our relationship with nature is forcing itself onto the agenda of any government. In a democracy these cannot remain purely technical problems; in the long run we would do better to be able to approach them from the standpoint of political principles which have won electoral support.

Global response to a global problem

Much of the preceding discussion is directed at existing and potential UK domestic policy, when in fact we are dealing with a global problem. Naturally, we must put our own house in order, but even there we won't get things right unless we keep reminding ourselves of the wider challenge of balancing global human development with the planet's natural capacity. Some of the decisions we must face can only be properly addressed internationally, such as the control of atmospheric carbon, or the distribution of world food resources.

No one can feel comfortable about this. Getting widely differing global interests to agree on any course of action is a heroic task. Much UK diplomacy, much statesmanship, much political capital has gone into the effort to reach workable agreements on carbon emissions and what progress has been made is greatly to our credit. What progress has been made, though, is painfully inadequate both in scope and pace. It is now 16 years since the Climate Convention was agreed at the Earth Summit, and its implementation through the Kyoto protocols has been faltering. World emissions of greenhouse gases continue to accelerate at an alarming rate.

Even when agreement can be reached, the means of implementation and enforcement are too weak. Given these obstacles it is easy and also rational to feel wholly pessimistic about our future. But if we choose optimism, and consider that there is at least good reason to strive for on ordered and intelligent global response to the present challenge on climate change and the future challenges on sustaining the global population in some sort of planetary balance, then it is obvious that this will require much stronger international institutions than we currently have.

Equally obviously, an apocalyptic outlook – that we are essentially unable to control our own development and are heading for a true ecological crash – will lead you to a different conclusion. But what if neither Apocalypse nor Utopia beckons? What if, in response to resource and population shocks, and probably much suffering, a less complacent world will need to seek stability in maintaining a collective balance with its resource base? Then, almost certainly, the need for strong global institutions will be obvious. The later they emerge, in fact, the longer the hard road will be.

Anyone who takes a global view of human ecology, therefore, has to be internationalist. It is not a sign of irrational optimism or wishful thinking; it is a rational approach to risk reduction. In this the instincts of traditional green politics towards insularity and self-sufficiency, the cause of all those gibes about yoghurt-knitting, are completely mistaken. Any true green politics must see globalisation as more opportunity than threat, because it opens the prospect of creating more effective institutions alongside open world markets.

So today, like our antecedents in the early Labour movement, we should seek strength in transnational and global collaboration. The three generations since the end of the 1939-45 war have seen the creation of a body of international law and a complex of international bodies – the three most significant of which are the UN, the World Trade Organisation and the European Union – which those Labour pioneers would have rejoiced in but which today are as likely to be a cause for scepticism and flight as enthusiasm and adherence. For all their faults, these institutions – and maybe others yet uncreated – are part of the framework within which we can grapple with the global challenge. Every step back from them, every year lost to insularity and scepticism, is a step back and a year lost in that part of our evolution which enables us to use our intelligence to adapt to global ecological pressures.

There is an obvious political pitfall here. A policy of vigorous engagement with – and strengthening of – transnational capacity can easily slide into one which distances decision-making from the electorate or creates mind-numbingly elaborate and unnecessary constraints on the life of the nation. The European Union has as often fallen into this error as it has risen to its nobler aims. This courts deserved unpopularity just as its successes justify its continuing reinforcement; people rightly dislike the loss of identity, be it national or any other sort, to homogenisation on matters of detail just as they recognise the value of the European settlement in wider political security and the guarantee of rights and freedoms.

The cure for this disease is basically a sense of proportion: be determinedly internationalist and build up the power of global institutions for the really global issues but do not allow them to use that power to invade the decisions which can and should be made at national level.

This does mean allocating 'sovereignty' to global rather than national levels; but sovereignty is not a fixed resource. The question is whether we, the electorate, in allowing governmental institutions at a range of levels to exercise authority on our behalf, are getting the most effective control of our communal resources and the right balance between collective obligation and individual freedom. Westminster's obsession with national sovereignty has been allowed to muddy our politics in this country for far too long.

You may think this is a sweeping, rhetorical way of dismissing the most vexed question of British politics of the last 30 years – on the right or the left. And of course you would be right; what this pamphlet is trying to do is to overview the whole landscape of policy to see what it looks like from the perspective of an ecological rationale, and that invites some generalisation.

But I am prepared to defend the rhetoric for three reasons. Firstly, that the 'problem' of sovereignty as it has been portrayed and developed in Britain is an evident obstacle to our chances of collective global action. Secondly, that it now feels wholly outdated, like worrying about the gold standard, and I'm bored to death with it. Please feel free to dismiss this as a purely personal expression of exasperation. I won't mind, and it isn't necessary to the argument; but, admit it, the prospect of another spat over the Maastricht treaty doesn't exactly set the blood racing.

And the third reason? That underneath what I have described as a sense of proportion is a solid principle which has been given quite considerable ethical and political underpinning already but goes by a wholly obscure name: subsidiarity. As with sustainability, it is a word I like to avoid if possible, but it is an essential principle for Labour if we wish to avoid one of the political risks to which I will return at the end of this pamphlet, that of the collective swamping the individual. It is interesting that it first appears in print, as far as I know, in the papal encyclical *Rerum Novarum* of 1891 , and it is a familiar political principle in many european countries, but here has been debased by being defined solely in terms of the repatriation of powers from Brussels to

Westminster.[27] This was a result of its incorporation into the Maastricht
Treaty. The current description is an update of that original treaty statement, now part of the Treaty of Nice:

> "The Community shall act within the limits of the powers conferred
> upon it by this Treaty and of the objectives assigned to it therein. In
> areas which do not fall within its exclusive competence, the Community
> shall take action, in accordance with the principle of subsidiarity, only if
> and in so far as the objectives of the proposed action cannot be suffi-
> ciently achieved by the Member States and can therefore, by reason of
> the scale or effects of the proposed action, be better achieved by the
> Community. Any action by the Community shall not go beyond what is
> necessary to achieve the objectives of this Treaty."[28]

But the principle is not a one-way street to devolution. In its pure form,
rather than its treaty form, it authorises collective action at any level
providing that it cannot be effectively taken at a lower one. In effect, it
is the application of devolution *upwards* in a society where the source of
all political authority is the individual and not the state. A proper understanding and application of this principle in the politics of the left would
go a long way to enable collective action at international level.[29]

My purpose here has been to illustrate that just as we cannot approach
an ecological politics in one country alone, so we cannot think of it
merely in scientific terms. The social and moral framework, the values
from which we derive our policy, are just as important. Seen purely as a
technical challenge for humanity as a whole, our response could fall
anywhere in the spectrum from absolute authoritarianism to social
primitivism depending on what values we bring to it. The history and
instincts of the left in Britain, and of Labour in particular, provide an
existing set of values which put the freedoms and opportunities of the
individual first, but see those freedoms and opportunities as being
universal rights which are advanced and buttressed by social, collective,
provisions and guarantees. This is an attractive starting point from

which to develop an electorally-successful set of principles which must have moral as well as scientific force.[30]

There seem to me to be two large ethical questions allied to the international aspects of the argument. One I have already alluded to: the building of political institutions beyond the state, which must also satisfy the demands of accountability and justice and do not erode but support individual rights and freedoms. The other is equity. This is not a new problem, of course, but it is given a new twist by the recognition that we have to plan our development sustainably because we can no longer believe or pretend that we can grow our way out of dealing with poverty by redistribution.

There can, indeed must, be growth – in food production, in health provision, in the availability of manufactured goods and so on. But we must also accept that an objective of international policy must be to bring about convergence in per capita consumption of natural resources, because there can be no rationale other than *force majeure* for some people to take to themselves a grossly inequitable share of the natural resource flows and assets of the planet.[31] This is why it is so vital for the developed world to accelerate its efforts to decouple wealth creation from natural resource consumption. But it also requires a politics which has championed the claims of the many against the few to extend its energy beyond national boundaries even at the risk of loss, given that in global terms our lifestyle puts us among the few, not among the many. We don't yet have this as a solid element in our electoral politics, though it may have been gaining some ground not least because of the personal convictions and actions of two New Labour Prime Ministers.

These moral arguments can be compelling in themselves. I, for one, would think so, and it is also true that moral purpose is what gives passion to politics and assures its relevance. When the electorate want to know what you stand for, 90 per cent of them are asking for your values not your manifesto. But this is no moral crusade. The actions we need to take, and the means we need to employ, are as clear an example of enlightened self-interest as any that could be found in the works of Adam Smith; but now expressed at the level of the global community as well as at the levels of the individual or the state.

Which brings me, before we close this section to look briefly, and I hope with distaste, at a common argument, if that is what it can be called, advanced by the climate change denial lobby, and heard in many a bar room parliament. This argument says that even if we were causing the problem, any action you or I may take will have so little impact that it is simply not worth taking; that the UK (substitute USA, or Europe – delete as appropriate) could incur large costs or impose large and unwelcome behavioural change, such as restricting the right to drive 4x4 s, and yet make a negligible impact on world emissions. Why should we suffer for no benefit?

Let us put aside the moral content, or lack of content, of this argument. The reason for taking action now, even at short-term cost, is enlightened self-interest to protect our standard of living and to make us better able to compete in the future – a future in which the triple pressures of population growth, natural resource constraint and the demand for equitable access to those resources are the forces that will shape our economy.

What does then matter is the balance between the cost of interventions and the value of the expected future benefits. This is a difficult area and we have already discussed the way in which Lord Stern has tried to frame it for our management of carbon emissions. I am certain that the economic methodology for these judgements will be a developing story for the foreseeable future, but it does underline one thing very strongly: that without the support of emerging international agreements these considerations become much more uncertain and difficult. The lesson is not that the national effort is pointless in the absence of international agreement, nor that international agreements are enough in themselves. It is that emerging international agreements deliver their benefit by reducing the present risks of national action.[32]

Biological resources

It is much easier to address how we might manage physical resources than biological ones, yet it is the management of the biosphere that will be the bigger long-term challenge. Its appearance at the end of this discussion is as a result of its complexity, not because of low priority, and also because the large scale issues involved will require the stronger international structures which were the subject of the preceding section.

We simply do not yet know enough to see how this challenge will be defined and then addressed. There are, presumably, thresholds below which the capacity of the biosphere to absorb the products of human activity fails, but what are they? Have we passed them or are they distant? Which elements of the life systems are the crucial ones, or is their functionality (from a human point of view) diffused through the whole system? How much genetic diversity is enough to prevent evolution stalling or to ensure we have a rich enough ecological resource for future human progress? Or to repeat a question I posed earlier, "How much wild does a world of nine billion human beings need?"

What we do know is that our dominance of the Earth's life systems is causing their biological capacity to fall at an alarming rate. So a policy of conservation is essential in our present state of knowledge. That state of knowledge is best summarised in the Millennium Ecosystem Assessments, which, after an exhaustive review of evidence on habitats, species and systems, came to a series of conclusions some of which I now quote.

- Everyone in the world depends on nature and ecosystem services to provide the conditions for a decent, healthy, and secure life.
- Humans have made unprecedented changes to ecosystems in recent decades...
- These changes have helped to improve the lives of billions, but at the same time they weakened nature's ability to deliver other key services such as purification of air and water, protection from disasters, and the provision of medicines.

50

- Human activities have taken the planet to the edge of a massive wave of species extinctions, further threatening our own well-being.
- Measures to conserve natural resources are more likely to succeed if local communities are given ownership of them, share the benefits, and are involved in decisions.
- Even today's technology and knowledge can reduce considerably the human impact on ecosystems. They are unlikely to be deployed fully, however, until ecosystem services cease to be perceived as free and limitless, and their full value is taken into account.
- Better protection of natural assets will require coordinated efforts across all sections of governments, businesses, and international institutions. The productivity of ecosystems depends on policy choices on investment, trade, subsidy, taxation, and regulation, among others.[33]

That, in a nutshell, is how we stand in relation to the biosphere. The message is stark but, compared to the political leverage that atmospheric carbon has got, backed by the scientific assessments of the IPCC, the MEA report has made little political impact. It should be enough, though, to convince us that we must start actively managing biological resources, and that a determined research effort is needed to better characterise the problems and to understand how that management might be made most effective.

In effect, natural processes have been replaced in well over half the planet's land ecosystems, by human ones. It is not too much of a metaphor to say that in these systems we have taken over responsibility for evolution from Nature. So far we have not proved ourselves up to the job; but our own progress now depends on using our intelligence at a species level to be good managers of our habitat. That means much greater knowledge of what we are doing in this managed environment and strong global agreements which enable it to be done; while at the same time taking care to preserve and ideally extend the unmanaged wild – those large scale habitats in which natural variation and selection still operates.

This is one of today's most pressing problems – the continued loss of wild habitat to exploitation, sometimes for agriculture, often for natural resources. As food production will have to increase to meet rising demand, there is a real risk that we will push the area of land under agriculture past the point at which the Natural habitats of the Earth cease to provide their system-wide functions and become mere museum pieces. So continuing to raise the efficiency of agricultural production is an ecological as well as an economic imperative.

This has significant implications for policy. For instance, if we accept our responsibility for the managed environment, we have to use all the tools at our disposal and our new-found ability to directly modify genes can be no exception, so outright opposition to the use of GM crops is in fact itself an ecological danger. The rational approach is to have a strong enough regulatory framework, both over the technology itself and its application to agricultural ecosystems, coupled with limits to the extent of commercial ownership of what, in our current circumstances, have to be seen as collectively owned properties.

Large-scale global nature conservation is therefore a strategic aim for the foreseeable future, and the creation of the machinery to secure it becomes urgent. This machinery must include international law to define the balance between the rights of nations and those of the human collective – the question of so-called 'global commons'. But what if anything does this mean for domestic conservation policy? On the one hand, the presumption for conservation remains the right policy given our present knowledge. On the other, if the management of our ecosystems becomes as central to the function of government as I believe it eventually will, we must expect it to become more sophisticated, allowing a dynamic system of habitat defence, maintenance, creation and surrender.

Even now, the focus of statutory conservation bodies is moving towards 'landscape-level' management when once it was all site and species protection.[34] Even now there is an understanding that not everything that is rare is necessarily precious. And given that the UK contains very little, if any, genuinely wild ecology, our main priority is the responsible management of our territory for biological richness and diversity and for the eco-system services and cultural value it provides.

The Green Crunch

4. What are the lessons for Labour?

This pamphlet starts with an observation – that humanity now needs to manage its place on the planet in order to sustain it – the simplicity of which hides what I believe to be profound challenges to the way we organise our society and the way we think about economics. The observation isn't original. Since I began to make these arguments in public speeches I have lost count of the number of people who say that they recognise and indeed find it hard to disagree with the diagnosis. What is much harder to identify is the cure.

The very depth of the ecological challenge may be the reason for so little progress having been made in meeting it; it is simply too difficult to see how politics can cope. In fact many people question whether world economic and political systems can adapt to such constraints. But of course they must, because the ecological forces will prevail and we will have to adapt. The question is whether we will adapt rapidly enough to control our future and forestall a series of painful readjustments or settle for picking up the pieces afterwards.

But I do think politics can change to engage with the challenge. The first and crucial step is to accept that ecological and natural resource management will be as important a task for Governments and parties as social and economic management are today; never mind that the consequences of this are not fully understood yet. We may still await the

Keynes of the economics of Nature, but we can see the main outlines of what we will have to grapple with.

Notice that I didn't say that the environment must join social and economic policy in the famous (and fatuous) 'three-legged stool' analogy. There is a semantic reason for this; when most people hear the word 'environment' they think of pollution control, wildlife conservation, farming and nowadays sometimes climate change. I hope that I have made it clear that the challenge is wider than any or all of these. But there is another structural reason. The analogy of three independent pillars of policy is a dangerous fallacy. In fact – and this is so obvious that it pains me to point it out – the economy takes place within human social structures, and human society exists within the physical and biological systems of the planet. This inclusivity is why, while the ecological envelope is loose enough, you can get away with considering economic policy (as we have done for most of the last 300 years) without worrying about ecological effects, but you cannot have a natural resource policy without worrying about economic effects.

When I talk about making that first step, I am not of course referring to the business of government but of electoral politics and the principles on which parties stand and which define their purpose. The people, not the political class, must define and demand this change and although they are unlikely to do so very quickly without political leadership, we are quite possibly at the point at which such leadership would find a positive response. As I have already pointed out, government is already becoming aware of what needs to be done and is finding some useful responses but is doing so despite rather than because of external political demand.

Accepting this wider definition then obliges a rethink about objectives or priorities in important areas of policy, many of which I have pointed out as the argument has unfolded. It is not like rewriting Clause 4, which was a largely symbolic action which gave dramatic form to changes already made as much as creating a new direction – though that was how it was meant to be seen by the electorate. No party, certainly not one in Government, could just change the sign above the door without restocking the shop.

In energy policy it means much more rapid decarbonisation, heavily incentivised by Government, probably a period of price control to stabilise investment behaviours and measures to preserve affordability for individual consumers. This could not be achieved without a much more closely regulated market.

But as we have seen, energy is not the only natural resource issue, just among the most urgent. The tools of government would need to expand to include measures of key resource flows, to develop indicators within the economy as a whole (and then probably at the level of the firm too) which would allow us pursue an objective of sharp reduction of the resource intensity of production in order to decouple wealth creation from resource depletion.[35]

Such a decoupling, achieved presumably over an extended period, would change the industrial structure of Britain, create and destroy jobs, require new technologies, products and processes to evolve. To ensure that the transitional social and economic costs are minimised and at the same time to maximise the competitive advantage that should accrue from this transition requires an explicit industrial strategy, or series of sectoral strategies.

Demand management, for instance through energy efficiency, and the closing of resource loops to avoid materials being discarded are also obvious components of the policy mix, and will require both the market price to reflect the real value of the resources concerned and structural incentives to enable change.

Our recent experience in this area – specifically in the reduction of carbon intensity through energy efficiency and the standards of the built environment – has made me think that we also have a problem with when we see the individual as citizen and when as consumer. For example, there are two routes to getting carbon reduction through more efficient buildings; you can just regulate for them, or you can persuade the consumer to demand them (by demanding high standards when buying a house, for instance) or to respond to incentives to provide them. This choice repeats itself in area after area; choice of car, retail packaging, carbon footprint of goods, etc. We got to the point at which Walker's crisp packets had a little logo on the back to tell you how many grams of carbon you are responsible for when you buy them, as if averting ecological damage were a matter of consumer choice. This is a category mistake, placing the decision on a matter of collective importance in the hands of the individual whose action is almost irrelevant, and is in conflict with the principle of subsidiarity. I mention this here, not to dismiss consumer choice or consumer power as a motive force for change, but to illustrate that my earlier advocacy for this principle is not just in application to international governance, and that it has consequences elsewhere too. In any event we have to be careful that consumer-based solutions are sought where they will be effective; not simply because we want to duck out of doing the rather harder political job of regulating.

Climate change is already a big political issue, and I have said much about that already. There is one notable feature of our response to climate change that I want to touch on in this summary, and that is the creation of a body which will set targets and examine progress towards them over a period much longer than the electoral cycle. This is an innovative move and one that is likely to be repeated, for we must find ways of agreeing and carrying out long-term programmes and policies in all these areas of resource management.

But it does risk cutting across the assumptions of party politics as we know it. The primacy of Parliament, its competency to take any action on the basis of a popular mandate, is an important part of our democracy. It has, however, enabled an over-simplified view of the world to be presented to the electorate especially during election campaigns. The reality is that political power is diffused by virtue of past decisions, made in the public interest, to vest decision-making in the courts or in a range of organs and agencies of the state, or, by treaty obligations, in extra-national bodies. Then, when these powers are used in ways which irritate the people or their elected representatives, the political response is to promise to take them back, and the airwaves fill with bonfires of the quangos, attacks on geriatric judges or threats to withdraw from Europe.

The creation of machinery such as the Climate Change Committee or the stronger transnational agreements which I have advocated as necessary to meet the global nature of the ecological challenge risk further complicating this already complex picture, disempowering elected representatives and increasing the sense that "they are all the same". There is no easy answer to this, but it does suggest to me that Labour should continue the existing shift from describing government as an exercise in command-and-control to one of ensuring accountability, and that it is right to place power at the level where it can most effectively be used for any given objective – the subsidiarity principle. That this will entail also recognising that certain tasks now undertaken by the national government should be reassigned *downwards* will help. If we are moving towards structures of government in which the national level – still, one assumes, the primary holder of the elected mandate – sits within a wider spectrum of bodies, from the global to the local, each having a cogent case for embodying some aspect of collective interest, then Labour could, rather unexpectedly, become a party which advocates small government, taken in the sense of its direct management functions, while at the same time having real clout through its ability to direct policy and ensure accountability.

But whatever structures of government emerge, the basic appeal to use politics to authorise collective action for the collective good is at the heart of the matter. This should be – is – natural Labour ground, and it is one that not only makes absolute sense in terms of enlightened self-interest in the face of ecological pressures but also one that has enduring appeal to the British electorate. Today that appeal to commonwealth, as the founders of our movement called it, has to encompass, much more strongly than it has in the past, other peoples and cultures, and incorporate them too into our notions of equality, because it is now clearer that our fortunes are linked; so it is not a return to the past but an evolution from it.

And in another way we must move on from our past, and learn from it. For the flip side of the collective principle in the past was statism and a lack of respect for individual opportunities and freedoms. Is it possible to have a politics which is both liberal and yet permits effective collective action? I think so, providing that we are prepared to start with the individual as the source of political authority and allocate that authority upwards where necessary into institutions which can respond to our common needs.

If we are thinking about the principles that define the left in Britain, we also have to examine our attitude to the consumer society. We are rightly proud of the achievements of Labour in securing material improvements in the lives of ordinary people. Quality of life has been lifted by material advancement as well by as social provision. But somewhere along the line western societies have first confused, and then substituted, quality if life with consumption, to the extent that the bellwether indicator of political success is GDP per head. There are – have always been – those who find this idea barbaric and choose to live by other lights, and there may be more people now who feel like this than there have been in recent generations. I am not, however, appealing here to a moral anti-materialism, but to two nearly irreconcilable truths. The first is that as we stand today the electorate has come to expect continued growth in purchasing power from its government's handling of the economy, and most people also define personal improvement in terms of increased ability to acquire goods. The second is that a continued increase in per capita consumption of natural resource is not possible, or not for long.

In these circumstances there are only two possible responses available to us. (I am excluding a new Puritanism, a politics of impoverishment.) We must quickly decouple material production from natural resource consumption so that a reasonable continued level of material improvement remains possible; and the quicker we can do this, the easier our other problems will become to resolve. Secondly, while we are doing this, we have to find ways of putting materialism in its place in our politics. We have to convince people of the nature of the problem and of the actions – some of which I have referred to in this pamphlet – that are needed for its resolution. In doing this our appeal is to our common interest as members of human communities who must begin to understand, at a global level, something our ancestors understood instinctively at a local one – how to live well in balance with nature. We cannot go back to that past and nor should we want to. We can leave romantic primitivism to the eco-warriors. Instead we look forward, to societies where the majority of the people are city-dwellers, in which we use the full range of human knowledge and technical skill in securing the common benefits of social, economic and ecological stability which are the necessary conditions for individual development and fulfilment. This is not Labour's ground by divine right, but neither is it so much different from the vision of our founders; which is why I believe that we are the best hope for those who want to build an ecologically responsible politics. But do we want to?

I finish with this challenge and this thought. Our species is extraordinary. Our whole existence occupies what amounts to the blink of an eye in the long history of life on this planet, yet we are –so far – its most successful and significant life form. Our individual intelligence gives us a natural ecological advantage but what has enabled our development to outstrip evolution has been what I might call our social intelligence – the ability to plan and to organise our societies to command the Earth's resources, the ability to learn collectively and to use our understanding collectively. We are, quite literally, a biological explosion. If it is this extraordinary intelligence that got us here so rapidly, the real test of that intelligence is whether we can now plan for our own sustainable existence within this possibly unique Earth system.

The Green Crunch

Afterword

I t's easy to be wise after the event. It's not much harder being wise before it, come to that. Diagnosis of our ecological problem isn't especially difficult, nor is speculation about some aspects of the future economy and society we should be aiming for if we want to live in balance with the economy of Nature. What is difficult is finding and following the path to that future in the real world of democratic politics.

This is what makes so many of the demands that the green movement makes of government – of all serious politicians – hard to take. There are many demands and almost all can sound like counsels of perfection. They fall, not so much on deaf ears, as on exasperated ones. Government hears a cacophony of voices offering undifferentiated advice but very little practical help. And like some *basso continuo* under it all, the tones of Private Fraser: "we're doomed, I tell you".

Yet the ecological challenge *is* a profound one and will not be disregarded. What should politicians do? Not some time in the future, but now? What actions can a concerned citizen reasonably hope for from elected leaders? What can those leaders hope to seek authority for? From where we are today to a sustainable human occupation of the Earth will be a long journey, only a little of which can be covered in the term of office of any government and not to recognise this disempowers the political process.

It seems to me that there are three fields for action for political leaders.

The first, and by far the most important, is to begin to make our relationship with Nature part of the core of political values and programmes. Do we yet have the Keir Hardie or the Emmeline Pankhurst who can both show people a vision of the future and recruit their support for it? For it is for politics as much as for science to bring both the problem and its resolution into sharper focus.

An ecologically intelligent politics cannot be smuggled past the electorate but will need their support; and to get that support will require more than the rationale offered today for action, which is essentially that we need to take some action over carbon because, if we don't, things will get a lot worse. A political movement cannot be built on the platform of making the best of a bad job. It will need principles of action, and the language to bring those principles to life. This pamphlet has attempted to isolate what some of those principles are; but in short, human sustainability has to be taken into the soul of politics.

Start, therefore, talking to the electorate about these things, in or out of elections. Start to use the principles to derive your policy. Call it 'stewardship', call it 'balance with Nature', call it 'solidarity', call it 'care for the future' – call it what you will so long as people can understand it (which probably rules out using the word 'sustainability') – but make it part of what drives political choices. Let people see where they are going.

The second field of action is to take the steps on that journey that are within your practical reach. That means focusing, as this pamphlet has, on carbon and energy policy as the most immediate issue in the politics of natural resource management, and in the medium term may include a range of other resource issues. That is why so much of this pamphlet has had to deal with what I called the economics of Nature, the first stage in which is to understand and manage the quantifiable exchanges of physical resources between the human species and the Earth system. In a relatively short span I have tried to indicate some of the practical policy challenges that arise from this.

Take the opportunities that events present; the unexpected and much unsought opportunity as 2009 begins is that of using the downturn with its destabilising consequences as a way of accelerating the change to a greener, more resource-efficient economy, which also serves the nation's long-term comparative advantage.

The third field of action is to equip ourselves better for the journey. To recognise what we don't know, yet need to know, to manage our relationship with the Earth systems (and to set about remedying that lack) will require a determined international research effort to bring economic and scientific insights alongside each other, both in the service of decision-making, and to create new ways of thinking about and understanding our place in the world.

That is an intellectual enterprise. Other re-equipping will be much less refined. For we also have to create the means by which either global actions can be authorised and taken, or national actions so co-ordinated as to come to much the same thing. We have to find the legal and institutional means to give binding reality to the facts of our interdependence.

John Harman
December 2008

The Green Crunch

References

1   I imagine there are some readers who are unfamiliar with that infallible indicator of American life and attitudes, The Simpsons. But the rest will recall Lisa's environmental presentation 'An Irritating Truth'. That's what I mean.

2   Janine Benyus' subject, Biomimicry, is the study of how we can design, for example, methods of production by analogy with natural processes and in sympathy with them. See *Biomimicry: Innovation Inspired by Nature*, Janine M. Benyus, HarperCollins, 2002.

3   www.wwf.org.uk/oneplanetliving

4   Herman Daly has been publishing in this field since the less 1970s which makes him something of a prophet. I couldn't find a place for the following quote in the text but couldn't resist adding it here: "Environmental degradation is an iatrogenic disease induced by economic physicians who treat the basic malady of unlimited wants by prescribing unlimited growth ... Yet one certainly does not cure a treatment-induced disease by increasing the treatment dosage." Key reading would be: *Ecological Economics: Principles And Applications* (with Joshua Farley) Island Press, 2003; *Valuing the Earth: Economics, Ecology, Ethics* (with Kenneth N. Townsend) MIT Press, 1993; *Beyond Growth: The Economics of Sustainable Development*, Beacon Press, 1997.

5   As is amply demonstrated by a recent report of the Carbon Trust, working with McKinsey & Co *Climate Change – A business revolution?* which identifies major industrial sectors where higher

performance would create significant increases in value. The report is at www.carbontrust.co.uk but be prepared to go through a strange registration procedure.

6   The Aldersgate Group (www.aldersgategroup.org.uk) is an alliance of businesses, NGOs and agencies which promotes the systemic economic benefits of high environmental standards. Its original report *Green Foundations* (2006) assembled some of the evidence for this and as this goes to print, the group is publishing an update, *Green Foundations 2009*.

7   Regulatory Enforcement and Sanctions Act 2008 (http://www.berr.gov.uk/whatwedo/bre/inspection-enforcement/implementing-principles/sanctions-bills/page44047.html)

8   I cant help reflecting that we owe this myopia in part to the lack of value accorded to science in the higher echelons of our society and the almost universal recruitment of policy advisors from educational backgrounds devoid of any scientific formation. It isn't by chance that the only Prime Minister in recent history to have had a scientific training, Margaret Thatcher, was the readiest, and earliest, to grasp the significance of the evidence on climate impacts.

9   www.hm-treasury.gov.uk/sternreview_index.htm

10   Most sensible demographic assessments project this as the world population by mid-century. The real issue is what rate of population growth we will have by then. Under some assumptions it might be reasonable to suppose that population might plateau at this sort of level. What seems certain is that world population won't level out below 9bn.

11   *A Pragmatic Energy Policy for the UK* Fell Associates 2008

12   For some years Ofgem had guidance on sustainable develop-
      ment but it was just that: guidance. It did not materially alter the
      price focus, nor was it meant to. The regulator now has, belat-
      edly, a sustainable development duty which has yet to prove itself
      significantly more effective than the guidance.

13   Energy White Paper 2007 (www.berr.gov.uk/whatwedo/energy/
      whitepaper/page39534.html)

14   Background to the Energy White Paper 2003 e.g.
      www.berr.gov.uk/files/file21350.pdf

15   my.barackobama.com/page/content/newenergy

16   At the time of writing, there is a discussion taking place in the
      European Commission as to what proportion of carbon can be
      bought in in this way, with considerable industrial pressure to
      raise that to a level which would effectively remove the power of
      the trading scheme to drive rapid industrial decarbonisation in
      Europe. The position of the UK Government in this is far from
      clear, but some commentary suggests that the proposition may
      be to allow 50 per cent of allocations to be so bought.

17   This is not the place for a closer study of carbon pricing, but it is
      worth noting that there are several carbon prices, widely
      different, and based on different valuations, in existence today.
      There is the implicit price of carbon in the oil price (market-based
      but cartel-led); there are prices created by regulated markets
      which are partly the result of policy choices, partly derived from
      trading; one is the EU trading price, another is that of CDM
      (Clean Development Mechanism) credits; there is Stern's "social

price of carbon" and there is, still under discussion, the "shadow price of carbon" which is to be used in government for policy evaluation. Try going on the web to buy carbon offsets and you will find a wide range of others.

18   See, for example *Unconventional Oil: Scraping the Bottom of the Barrel* (WWF/Co-operative Bank 2008) www.assets.wwf.org.uk/downloads/scraping_barrell.pdf

19   There is another golden rule, and it goes right to the heart of the problem. Ecologists think about resources habitually in terms of cycles, interdependencies, feedback. Economics tends to treat resources as passing through the economy in a linear process. If I had to give this pamphlet the Reduced Shakespeare Company treatment and boil it down to a single phrase it would be the "pursuit of health, wealth and happiness within the Earth's natural cycles". It is interesting to see that the Chinese are now using the term 'circular economy' in relation to resource management.

20   I should declare some partiality here, having been the co-chairman of the Sustainable Building Task Force which proposed the Code in 2004. It covers a range of environmental aspects of the design and construction of homes, including energy and water efficiency; but not yet the use of materials in construction or the management of waste.

21   The phrases are especially associated with the Wuppertal Institute. There is plenty of good reference material at www.wupperinst.org/FactorFour (and it is in English)

22   www.defra.gov.uk/environment/business/commission/index.htm

23   I have made this sentence deliberately unconstitutional. It is

Parliament which holds Government to account; of course. The committee provides the commentary with which this can be done. But the mechanism is described as a direct holding to account more often than not.

24 Until the last two Chief Scientists, Sir Robert May and Sir David King, took the bull by the horns and drove the reality of the science home.

25 I have given only the barest summary in the text, which rather underplays the serious content of the forecasts. More detail can be found at the websites of the Hadley Centre of the Met Office, one of the world's leading centres for climate science (www.metoffice.gov.uk/research/hadleycentre) and at that of the UK Climate Impacts Programme (www.ukcip.org.uk) which also gives a much wider account of adaptation issues than has been possible here.

26 For reasons of space I have said little elsewhere about agriculture but I do not want to convey the idea that the industry is marginal to these arguments. There is an adaptation challenge for the industry, but there are two bigger ones related very obviously to resource management (including food security) and ecological balance. The relationship between land and people has always been part of the bedrock of politics, and may now be regaining an importance which has been lost in the socio-economic era.

27 And was further developed in later encyclical *Quadragesima Anno* – literally the 40th anniversary of the first – with the following ringing declaration "... it is an injustice, a grave evil, and a disturbance of right order, for a larger and higher association to arrogate to itself functions that can be performed efficiently by smaller and lower societies. This is a fundamental

principle of social philosophy ..." I include this passage because it illustrates forcefully that our response to what seems a technical/scientific problem requiring a collective solution has to be founded on social and moral principles as well as scientific ones.

28   And also appeared as an article of the now-abandoned EU Constitution: "Under the principle of subsidiarity, in areas which do not fall within its exclusive competence the Union shall act only if and insofar as the objectives of the intended action cannot be sufficiently achieved by the Member States, either at central level or at regional and local level, but can rather, by reason of the scale or effects of the proposed action, be better achieved at Union level."

29   Although British politics has never come close; the only period in which the baffling word 'subsidiarity' issued readily from the lips of ministers was in the post-Maastricht grab to bring powers back to Westminster. I was a council leader at the time and remember asking whether the principle would be applied also to devolve powers from Westminster to Town Halls. Oddly enough, it wasn't.

30   Or should be. Sometimes we have let it morph into its ugly sister, statist, overweening and bureaucratic, forgetting that the collective is there to promote the interests of the individual rather than the other way round.

31   I use this term in its general sense, but also draw attention to the policy of 'Contraction and Convergence' advanced *inter alia* by the Global Commons Institute as a rational framework for international resource policy. See www.gci.org.uk.

32   Here is a good example showing how this is already a practical consideration, taken from the present set of expert commentaries

on the issues surrounding the setting of a shadow price for carbon. "This damage to the UK economy will depend on whether other countries adopt a similar stance. It is only worth adopting a stringent mitigation target ... if it is believed that at some point (perhaps some years after the UK) other countries will follow suit." (Paul Ekins) National action may be rational in the absence of international agreement but may also depend on the expectation of future international agreement (or of expected changes in international conditions.

33   Produced by a collaborative international science process working between 2001-5. See www.millenniumassessment.org.

34   See, for example, www.naturalengland.org.uk/research/policy-position-statements/docs/landscape-pps.pdf.

35   As I was writing this, the Prime Minister announced a reshuffle in which a new Department for Energy and Climate Change was created. Government structures are probably the least important bit of all this, but it would make great sense either to widen its brief to include all natural resource accounting, or to allocate that role to the Treasury.

The Green Crunch

Discussion Guide: The Green Crunch

FABIAN SOCIETY

The Green Crunch
Why we need a new economics for Britain's
environmental challenge
Sir John Harman

The new environmental challenge to British politics

'The Green Crunch: Why we need a new economics for Britain's environmental challenge' by Sir John Harman

How to use this Discussion Guide
The guide can be used in various ways by Fabian Local Societies, local political party meetings and trade union branches, student societies, NGOs and other groups.

- You might hold a discussion among local members or invite a guest speaker – for example, an MP, academic or local practitioner to lead a group discussion.

- Four different key themes are suggested. You might choose to spend 15 – 20 minutes on each area, or decide to focus the whole discussion on one of the issues for a more detailed discussion.

A discussion could address some or all of the following questions:

1 The economic challenges

The pamphlet argues for a 'new economics' which recognise how environmental constraints now limit our economic activity.

- How could a recession help or hinder the forging of a greener economy?

- What policy areas should governments prioritise to manage the transition to an ecologically sustainable economy?

2. The public politics of climate change

The pamphlet argues that a consensus at Westminster will not be enough if Jeremy Clarkson still has the ear of the electorate. But the author also argues that the electorate is aware that there is a problem, but does not yet see that a convicing set of remedies have been offered.

- How far have public attitudes shifted – and what are the most difficult barriers to the scale of change required?

- Which approaches to changing attitudes are most likely to be effective, and which could fail or backfire? Can you identify positive or negative lessons from major shifts in public attitudes, on the environment or other social issues?

- Is it possible to change ideas about 'quality of life' away from being measured so heavily by the values of a 'consumer society'? How could that be done in practice – and who can influence this most?

In discussing these issues, you might want to also consider who is most likely to be successful in influencing public attitudes and behaviour. For example, are there specific areas where you believe lead responsibility should belong to a particular group: such as national politicians, local government, business, the media, academic and scientific experts, schools, parents, individual citizens? What practical changes could they make to shift attitudes?

3. The challenges to Labour

The pamphlet argues that all political parties must rise to these challenges. The author also argues that Labour should be the party best placed to respond to environmental concerns, since the fundamental instincts and strengths of the Labour movement – equality, collectivism, internationalism – make it the most promising political vehicle for an effective response. You might want to discuss the challenges of creating a distinctive Labour argument in this area.

- What are the key arguments and messages which could make the environment part of Labour's core vision and narrative? How should the argument be made in a way which could engage and convince voters – for example in a General Election manifesto and campaign?

- What one or two key manifesto policies could best capture and signpost the broader environmental and economic strategy?

Groundwork seeks to change lives by working with communities in some of the most deprived areas of the country, to address the particular problems they face. We tackle urban blight and decay through greening up desolate and neglected places, making communities safer and healthier. But since regeneration is as much about people as it is about place, much of our work tackles social difficulties such as worklessness, health awareness and anti social behaviour.

CHANGING PLACES
CHANGING **LIVES**

Tony Hawkhead, Chief Executive of Groundwork

"We are delighted to be supporting this Fabian pamphlet and this important debate. The people we work with every day will see their communities suffer the most during recession and we'd like to see more opportunities for economic renewal directed towards them.

Politicians and economists are now trying to figure out what we need to do to ensure our society can withstand economic shock in future. A society which is more economically resilient is, by definition, one that is more sustainable. Recession could be used as a springboard – taking many of our communities from the post-industrial to the sustainable age.

This pamphlet promotes the debate we want politicians in all political parties to address. It is a valuable tool for those of us wanting a new kind of political emphasis with the environment and sustainability at its heart."

During the past year, Groundwork generated and invested £108 million in 6,000 practical projects to support regeneration and promote sustainable development in many of the country's most deprived areas. Our integrated approach means we seek to find ways of tackling social, economic and environmental problems together.

For more information on the projects we deliver, go to:
www.groundwork.org.uk.

Join Britain's only membership-based think tank

Join the Fabian Society and receive a free copy of 'Narrowing the Gap', worth £9.95, **plus** the Fabian Review environment special issue, **plus** the next two Fabian pamphlets. Call 020 7227 4900 or email us at info@fabian-society.org.uk for more information.

Fabian Review

LABOUR PARTY CONFERENCE ISSUE

www.fabians.org.uk

Autumn 2008

MUST LABOUR LOSE?

THE PROGRESSIVE FIGHTBACK

PETER KELLNER: Labour's glimmers of hope | **DAVID LAMMY:** Britain is not broken
STELLA CREASY: Connect like Obama | **JON TRICKETT:** Messages for the marginals
JAMES PURNELL: Rediscover redistribution | **FIONA MACTAGGART:** Tax like we mean it
TIM HORTON: The Conservatives' confusion

The quarterly magazine of the Fabian Society   Volume 119 no 4   £4.95

The Fabian Review, Spring 2008

British Muslims and the politics of fairness

In 'Fairness not Favours', Sadiq Khan MP argues that an effective agenda to provide opportunity and tackle extremism across all communities must go beyond a narrow approach to security, and sets out new proposals for a progressive agenda on inequality and life chances, public engagement in foreign policy, an inclusive Britishness, and rethinking the role of faith in public life.

The pamphlet puts the case for an effective agenda to provide opportunity and tackle extremism across all communities must go beyond a narrow approach to security, and sets out new proposals for a progressive agenda on inequality and life chances, public engagement in foreign policy, an inclusive Britishness, and rethinking the role of faith in public life.

85

Special offer: join the Fabians for just £9.95 and get this book free.

'The Fabians ask the most difficult questions, pushing Labour to make a bold, progressive case on taxation and the abolition of child poverty.' – Polly Toynbee

FABIAN SOCIETY

Narrowing the Gap
The Fabian Commission on Life Chances and Child Poverty

How can we make poverty history at home?

One in five children still grows up in poverty in Britain. Yet all the political parties now claim to care about 'social justice'. This report sets a litmus test by which Brown, Cameron and Campbell must be judged.

'Narrowing the Gap' is the final report of the Fabian Commission on Life Chances and Child Poverty, chaired by Lord Victor Adebowale. The Fabian Society is the only think tank with members. Join us and help us put poverty and equality at the centre of the political agenda.

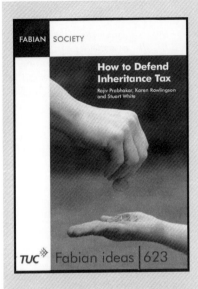

How to defend inheritance tax

Inheritance tax is under attack, and not just from the political right. The critics of this tax have dominated the debate over recent years but, as the authors of 'How to Defend Inheritance Tax' argue, this tax is one of the best tools we have for tackling inequality and kick starting Britain's stalled social mobility.

Defending inheritance tax is not just the responsibility of politicians – there must be a citizen-led campaign too. In this Fabian Ideas pamphlet, **Rajiv Prabhakar, Karen Rowlingson and Stuart White** provide progressives with the tools they need to win this argument.

They set out the evidence on inheritance and inequality, tackle the common objections to the tax, and demonstrate the moral and pragmatic arguments for an inheritance tax.

The Green Crunch

JOIN THE FABIANS TODAY
Join us and receive two Fabian Reviews, plus our award-winning equality report, 'Narrowing the Gap'

I'd like to become a Fabian for just £9.95

I understand that should at any time during my six-month introductory membership period I wish to cancel, I will receive a refund and keep all publications received without obligation. After six months I understand my membership will revert to the annual rate as published in *Fabian Review*, currently £33 (ordinary) or £16 (unwaged).

Name	Date of birth

Address

	Postcode

Email

Telephone

Instruction to Bank   Originator's ID: 971666

Bank/building society name

DIRECT Debit

Address

	Postcode

Acct holder(s)

Acct no.	Sort code

I instruct you to pay direct debits from my account at the request of the Fabian Society. The instruction is subject to the safeguards of the Direct Debit Guarantee.

Signature	Date

Return to:
Fabian Society Membership
FREEPOST SW 1570
11 Dartmouth Street
London
SW1H 9BN